SIXTH EDITION

Includes USB Flash Drive! *with 240 select MP3 Backing Tracks*

SIXTH EDITION

ISBN: 978-1-4768-7726-6

7777 W. BLUEMOUND RD. P.O. BOX 13819 MILWAUKEE, WI 53213

For all works contained herein:
Unauthorized copying, arranging, adapting, recording or public performance is an infringement of copyright.
Infringers are liable under the law.

Visit Hal Leonard Online at
www.halleonard.com

PREFACE

<u>The Real Book</u> is the answer to the fake book. It is an alternative to the plethora of poorly designed, illegible, inaccurate, badly edited volumes which abound on the market today. <u>The Real Book</u> is extremely accurate, neat, and is designed, above all, for practical use. Every effort has been made to make it enjoyable to play. Here are some of the primary features:

1. <u>FORMAT</u>
   a. The book is professionally copied and meticulously checked for accuracy in melody, harmony, and rhythms.
   b. Form within each tune, including both phrases and larger sections, is clearly delineated and placed in obvious visual arrangement.
   c. All two-page tunes open to face one another.
   d. Most standard-type tunes remain true to their original harmonies with little or no reharmonization. The exceptions include a handful of jazz interpretations of popular songs and Broadway showtunes, as well as some modifications using modern notation and variation among turnarounds.

2. <u>SELECTION OF TUNES AND EDITING</u>
   a. Major jazz composers of the last 60 years are highlighted, with special attention given to the 1960s and 1970s.
   b. While some commonly played tunes are absent from the book, many of the classics are here, including bop standards and a fine selection of Duke Ellington masterpieces.
   c. Many of the included arrangements represent the work of the jazz giants of the last 40 years – Miles, Coltrane, Shorter, Hancock, Evans, Mingus and Monk, as well as a variety of newer artists.
   d. A variety of recordings and alternate editions were consulted to create the most accurate and user-friendly representations of the tunes, whether used in a combo setting or as a solo artist.

3. <u>SOURCE REFERENCE</u>
   a. The composer(s) of every tune is listed.
   b. Every song presented in the Real Book is now fully licensed for use.

<u>Sixth Edition</u>
As we ventured into the 21st century, the same Real Book that has served us so graciously for the last 30 years was in need of a facelift. This new edition contains tunes that are re-arranged, re-transcribed and most importantly, licensed, so that you may study and play these works more accurately and legally. Enjoy!

A

AFRICAN FLOWER	10
AFRO BLUE	11
AFTERNOON IN PARIS	12
AGUA DE BEBER (WATER TO DRINK)	14
AIREGIN	13
ALFIE	16
ALICE IN WONDERLAND	17
ALL BLUES	18
ALL BY MYSELF	19
ALL OF ME	20
ALL OF YOU	21
ALL THE THINGS YOU ARE	22
ALRIGHT, OKAY, YOU WIN	24
ALWAYS	23
ANA MARIA	26
ANGEL EYES	28
ANTHROPOLOGY	29
APPLE HONEY	30
APRIL IN PARIS	32
APRIL JOY	33
ARISE, HER EYES	34
ARMAGEDDON	36
AU PRIVAVE	37
AUTUMN IN NEW YORK	38
AUTUMN LEAVES	39

B

BEAUTIFUL LOVE	40
BEAUTY AND THE BEAST	41
BESSIE'S BLUES	42
BEWITCHED	43
BIG NICK	44
BLACK COFFEE	45
BLACK DIAMOND	46
BLACK NARCISSUS	47
BLACK NILE	48
BLACK ORPHEUS	49

B Cont.

BLUE BOSSA	50
BLUE IN GREEN	51
BLUE MONK	52
THE BLUE ROOM	53
BLUE TRAIN	54
BLUES FOR ALICE	55
BLUESETTE	56
BODY AND SOUL	57
BOPLICITY	58
BRIGHT SIZE LIFE	59
BROAD WAY BLUES	60
BROADWAY	61
BUT BEAUTIFUL	62
BUTTERFLY	63
BYRD LIKE	64

C

C'EST SI BON (IT'S SO GOOD)	65
CALL ME	66
CALL ME IRRESPONSIBLE	67
CAN'T HELP LOVIN' DAT MAN	68
CAPTAIN MARVEL	70
CENTRAL PARK WEST	69
CEORA	72
CHEGA DE SAUDADE (NO MORE BLUES)	74
CHELSEA BELLS	73
CHELSEA BRIDGE	76
CHEROKEE (INDIAN LOVE SONG)	77
CHERRY PINK AND APPLE BLOSSOM WHITE	78
A CHILD IS BORN	79
CHIPPIE	80
CHITLINS CON CARNE	81
COME SUNDAY	82
COMO EN VIETNAM	83
CON ALMA	84
CONCEPTION	86

C Cont.

CONFIRMATION	87
CONTEMPLATION	88
CORAL	89
COTTON TAIL	90
COULD IT BE YOU	91
COUNTDOWN	92
CRESCENT	93
CRYSTAL SILENCE	94

D

D NATURAL BLUES	95
DAAHOUD	96
DANCING ON THE CEILING	98
DARN THAT DREAM	99
DAY WAVES	100
DAYS AND NIGHTS WAITING	101
DEAR OLD STOCKHOLM	102
DEARLY BELOVED	103
DEDICATED TO YOU	104
DELUGE	106
DESAFINADO	108
DESERT AIR	110
DETOUR AHEAD	105
DEXTERITY	112
DIZZY ATMOSPHERE	113
DJANGO	114
DOIN' THE PIG	116
DOLORES	118
DOLPHIN DANCE	119
DOMINO BISCUIT	120
DON'T BLAME ME	121
DON'T GET AROUND MUCH ANYMORE	122
DONNA LEE	123
DREAM A LITTLE DREAM OF ME	124
DREAMSVILLE	125

E

EASTER PARADE	126
EASY LIVING	127
EASY TO LOVE	128

E Cont.

ECCLUSIASTICS	129
EIGHTY ONE	130
EL GAUCHO	131
EPISTROPHY	132
EQUINOX	133
EQUIPOISE	134
E.S.P.	135

F

FALL	136
FALLING GRACE	137
FALLING IN LOVE WITH LOVE	138
FEE-FI-FO-FUM	139
A FINE ROMANCE	140
500 MILES HIGH	141
502 BLUES	142
FOLLOW YOUR HEART	143
FOOTPRINTS	144
FOR ALL WE KNOW	145
FOR HEAVEN'S SAKE	146
(I LOVE YOU) FOR SENTIMENTAL REASONS	147
FOREST FLOWER	148
FOUR	149
FOUR ON SIX	150
FREDDIE FREELOADER	151
FREEDOM JAZZ DANCE	152
FULL HOUSE	154

G

GEE BABY, AIN'T I GOOD TO YOU	153
GEMINI	156
GIANT STEPS	157
THE GIRL FROM IPANEMA	158
GLORIA'S STEP	159
GOD BLESS' THE CHILD	160
GOLDEN LADY	161
GOOD EVENING MR. AND MRS. AMERICA	162

G Cont.

GRAND CENTRAL	164
THE GREEN MOUNTAINS	165
GROOVIN' HIGH	166
GROW YOUR OWN	167
GUILTY	168
GYPSY IN MY SOUL	169

H

HALF NELSON	170
HAVE YOU MET MISS JONES?	172
HEAVEN	173
HEEBIE JEEBIES	174
HELLO, YOUNG LOVERS	176
HERE'S THAT RAINY DAY	175
HOT TODDY	178
HOUSE OF JADE	179
HOW HIGH THE MOON	180
HOW INSENSITIVE	181
HOW MY HEART SINGS	182
HULLO BOLINAS	183

I

I CAN'T GET STARTED WITH YOU	184
I CAN'T GIVE YOU ANYTHING BUT LOVE	185
I COULD WRITE A BOOK	186
I GOT IT BAD AND THAT AIN'T GOOD	187
I LET A SONG GO OUT OF MY HEART	188
I LOVE PARIS	189
I LOVE YOU	190
I MEAN YOU	191
I REMEMBER CLIFFORD	192
I SHOULD CARE	194
I WISH I KNEW HOW IT WOULD FEEL TO BE FREE	195
I'LL NEVER SMILE AGAIN	196
I'LL REMEMBER APRIL	197
I'M ALL SMILES	198
I'M BEGINNING TO SEE THE LIGHT	200
I'M YOUR PAL	201
ICARUS	202
IF YOU NEVER COME TO ME	204

I Cont.

IMPRESSIONS	205
IN A MELLOW TONE	206
IN A SENTIMENTAL MOOD	207
IN THE MOOD	208
IN THE WEE SMALL HOURS OF THE MORNING	210
IN YOUR QUIET PLACE	211
THE INCH WORM	212
INDIAN LADY	213
INNER URGE	214
INTERPLAY	215
THE INTREPID FOX	216
INVITATION	217
IRIS	218
IS YOU IS, OR IS YOU AIN'T (MA' BABY)	220
ISN'T IT ROMANTIC?	219
ISOTOPE	222
ISRAEL	223
IT DON'T MEAN A THING (IF IT AIN'T GOT THAT SWING)	224
IT'S EASY TO REMEMBER	225

J

JELLY ROLL	226
JORDU	227
JOURNEY TO RECIFE	228
JOY SPRING	229
JUJU	230
JUMP MONK	232
JUNE IN JANUARY	231
JUST ONE MORE CHANCE	234

K

KELO	236

L

LADY BIRD	235
LADY SINGS THE BLUES	238
LAMENT	239
LAS VEGAS TANGO	240

L Cont.

LAZY BIRD	241
LAZY RIVER	242
LIKE SOMEONE IN LOVE	243
LIMEHOUSE BLUES	244
LINES AND SPACES	246
LITHA	248
LITTLE BOAT	245
LITTLE WALTZ	250
LONG AGO (AND FAR AWAY)	251
LONNIE'S LAMENT	252
LOOK TO THE SKY	253
LOVE IS THE SWEETEST THING	254
LUCKY SOUTHERN	255
LULLABY OF BIRDLAND	256
LUSH LIFE	258

M

THE MAGICIAN IN YOU	257
MAHJONG	260
MAIDEN VOYAGE	261
A MAN AND A WOMAN	262
MAN IN THE GREEN SHIRT	264
MEDITATION	266
MEMORIES OF TOMORROW	267
MICHELLE	268
MIDNIGHT MOOD	269
MIDWESTERN NIGHTS DREAM	270
MILANO	272
MINORITY	273
MISS ANN	274
MISSOURI UNCOMPROMISED	275
MR. P.C.	276
MISTY	277
MIYAKO	278
MOMENT'S NOTICE	280
MOOD INDIGO	279
MOONCHILD	282
THE MOST BEAUTIFUL GIRL IN THE WORLD	283
MY BUDDY	284
MY FAVORITE THINGS	285
MY FOOLISH HEART	286

M Cont.

MY FUNNY VALENTINE	287
MY ONE AND ONLY LOVE	288
MY ROMANCE	289
MY SHINING HOUR	290
MY SHIP	291
MY WAY	292
MYSTERIOUS TRAVELLER	294

N

NAIMA	293
NARDIS	296
NEFERTITI	297
NEVER WILL I MARRY	298
NICA'S DREAM	299
NIGHT DREAMER	300
THE NIGHT HAS A THOUSAND EYES	301
A NIGHT IN TUNISIA	302
NIGHT TRAIN	304
NOBODY KNOWS YOU WHEN YOU'RE DOWN AND OUT	303
NOSTALGIA IN TIMES SQUARE	306
NUAGES	307

O

(OLD MAN FROM) THE OLD COUNTRY	308
OLEO	309
OLILOQUI VALLEY	310
ONCE I LOVED	311
ONCE IN LOVE WITH AMY	312
ONE FINGER SNAP	313
ONE NOTE SAMBA	314
ONLY TRUST YOUR HEART	315
ORBITS	316
ORNITHOLOGY	317
OUT OF NOWHERE	318

P

PAPER DOLL	319
PASSION DANCE	320

P Cont.

PASSION FLOWER 321
PEACE 322
PEGGY'S BLUE SKYLIGHT 323
PENT UP HOUSE 324
PENTHOUSE SERENADE 325
PERI'S SCOPE 326
PFRANCING (NO BLUES) 327
PINOCCHIO 328
PITHECANTHROPUS ERECTUS 329
PORTSMOUTH FIGURATIONS 330
PRELUDE TO A KISS 331
PRINCE OF DARKNESS 332
P.S. I LOVE YOU 333
PUSSY CAT DUES 334

Q

QUIET NIGHTS OF QUIET STARS
    (CORCOVADO) 335
QUIET NOW 336

R

RECORDA-ME 337
RED CLAY 338
REFLECTIONS 340
REINCARNATION OF A LOVEBIRD 342
RING DEM BELLS 341
ROAD SONG 344
'ROUND MIDNIGHT 345
RUBY, MY DEAR 346

S

THE SAGA OF HARRISON
    CRABFEATHERS 348
SATIN DOLL 349
SCOTCH AND SODA 350
SCRAPPLE FROM THE APPLE 351
SEA JOURNEY 352
SEVEN COME ELEVEN 354
SEVEN STEPS TO HEAVEN 356
SIDEWINDER 355

S Cont.

SILVER HOLLOW 358
SIRABHORN 359
SKATING IN CENTRAL PARK 360
SO NICE (SUMMER SAMBA) 362
SO WHAT 364
SOLAR 363
SOLITUDE 366
SOME DAY MY PRINCE WILL COME 367
SOME OTHER SPRING 368
SOME SKUNK FUNK 370
SOMEBODY LOVES ME 369
SOMETIME AGO 372
SONG FOR MY FATHER 373
THE SONG IS YOU 374
SOPHISTICATED LADY 376
THE SORCERER 377
SPEAK NO EVIL 378
THE SPHINX 379
STANDING ON THE CORNER 380
THE STAR-CROSSED LOVERS 381
STELLA BY STARLIGHT 382
STEPS 383
STOLEN MOMENTS 384
STOMPIN' AT THE SAVOY 385
STRAIGHT NO CHASER 386
A STRING OF PEARLS 388
STUFF 390
SUGAR 387
A SUNDAY KIND OF LOVE 392
THE SURREY WITH THE
    FRINGE ON TOP 393
SWEDISH PASTRY 394
SWEET GEORGIA BRIGHT 395
SWEET HENRY 396

T

TAKE FIVE 397
TAKE THE "A" TRAIN 398
TAME THY PEN 400
TELL ME A BEDTIME STORY 402
THANKS FOR THE MEMORY 399
THAT'S AMORE 404

T Cont.

THERE IS NO GREATER LOVE 406
THERE WILL NEVER BE
        ANOTHER YOU 407
THERE'LL BE SOME CHANGES MADE 408
THEY DIDN'T BELIEVE ME 409
THINK ON ME 410
THOU SWELL 411
THREE FLOWERS 412
TIME REMEMBERED 413
TONES FOR JOAN'S BONES 414
TOPSY 415
TOUR DE FORCE 416
TRISTE 417
TUNE UP 418
TURN OUT THE STARS 419
TWISTED BLUES 420

U

UNCHAIN MY HEART 422
UNIQUITY ROAD 421
UNITY VILLAGE 424
UP JUMPED SPRING 425
UPPER MANHATTAN
        MEDICAL GROUP 426

V

VALSE HOT 427
VERY EARLY 428
VIRGO 429

W

WAIT TILL YOU SEE HER 430
WALTZ FOR DEBBY 432
WAVE 431
WE'LL BE TOGETHER AGAIN 434
WELL YOU NEEDN'T 435
WEST COAST BLUES 436
WHAT AM I HERE FOR? 437
WHAT WAS 438
WHEN I FALL IN LOVE 439
WHEN SUNNY GETS BLUE 440

W Cont.

WHEN YOU WISH UPON A STAR 441
WHISPERING 442
WILD FLOWER 444
WINDOWS 443
WITCH HUNT 446
WIVES AND LOVERS 448
WOODCHOPPER'S BALL 447
WOODYN' YOU 450
THE WORLD IS WAITING
        FOR THE SUNRISE 451

Y

YES AND NO 452
YESTERDAY 453
YESTERDAYS 454
YOU ARE THE SUNSHINE
        OF MY LIFE 456
YOU ARE TOO BEAUTIFUL 455
YOU BROUGHT A NEW KIND
        OF LOVE TO ME 458
YOU DON'T KNOW WHAT LOVE IS 459
YOU TOOK ADVANTAGE OF ME 460
YOUNG AT HEART 461
YOU'RE NOBODY 'TIL SOMEBODY
        LOVES YOU 462

D.S. for solos
After solos, D.S. al ⊕

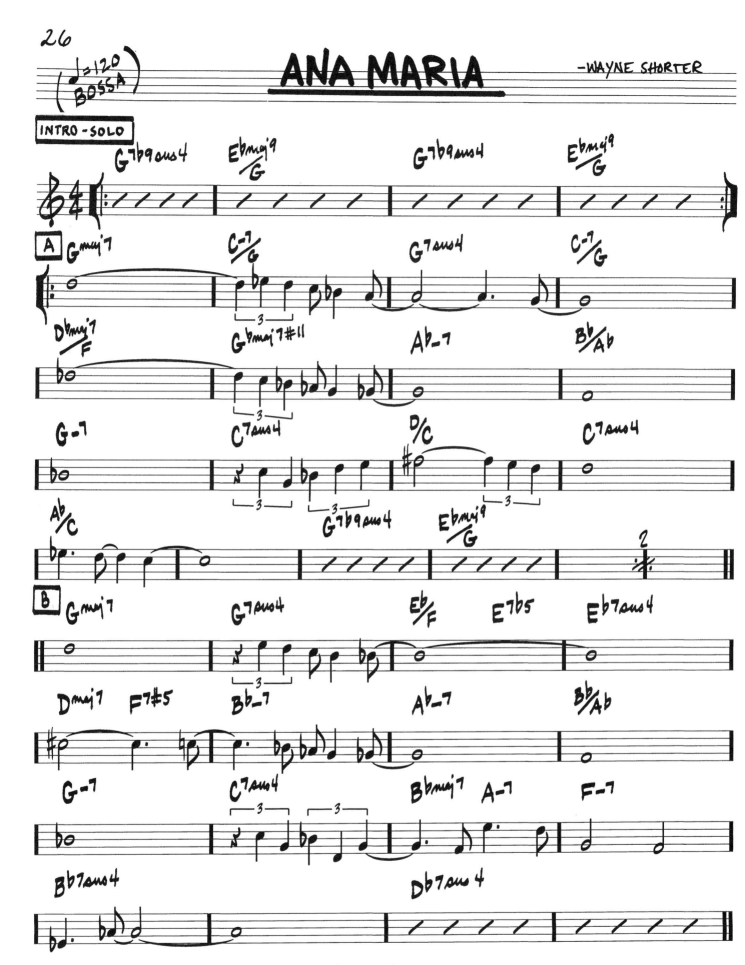

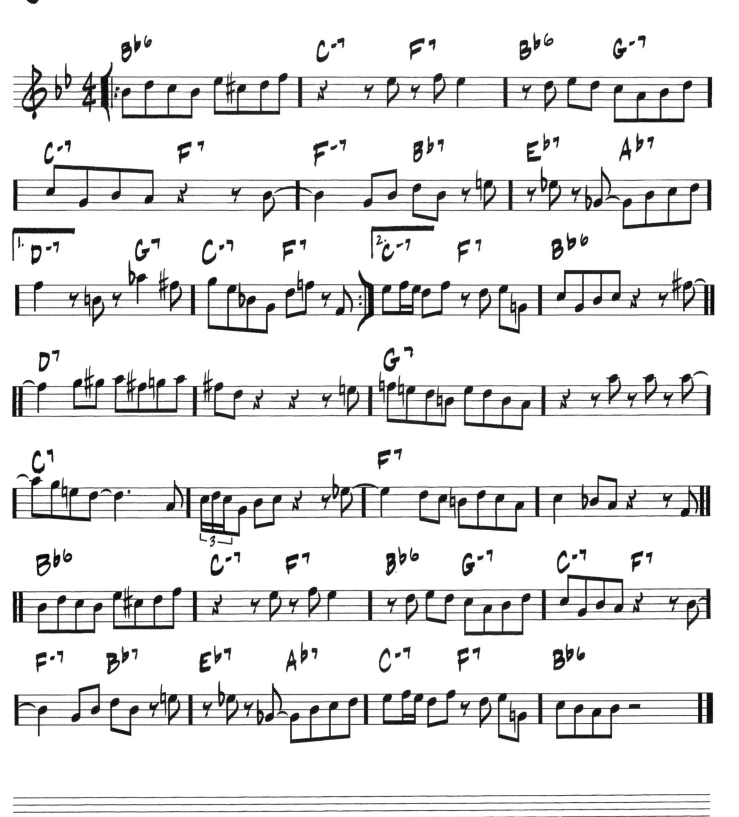

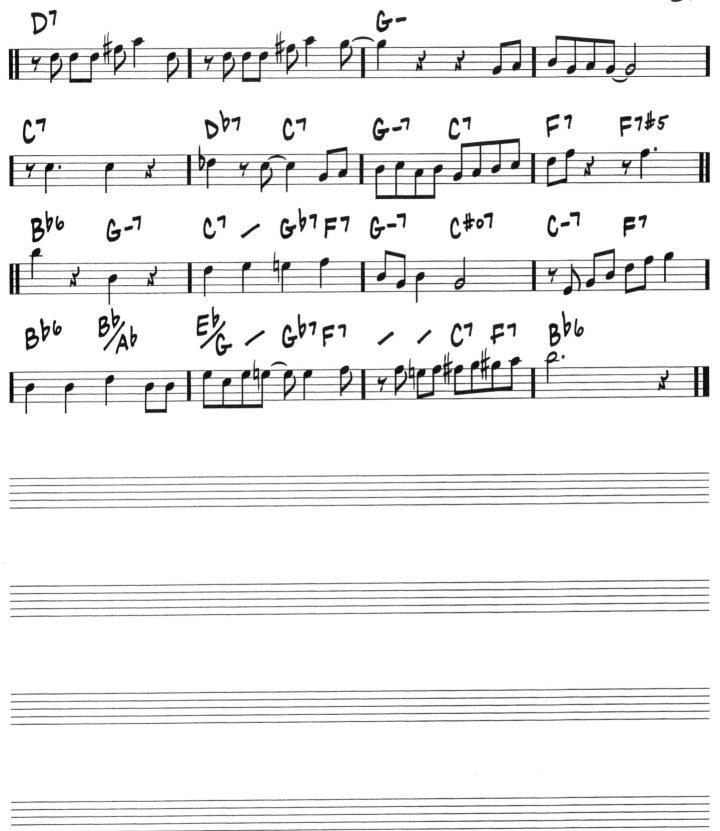

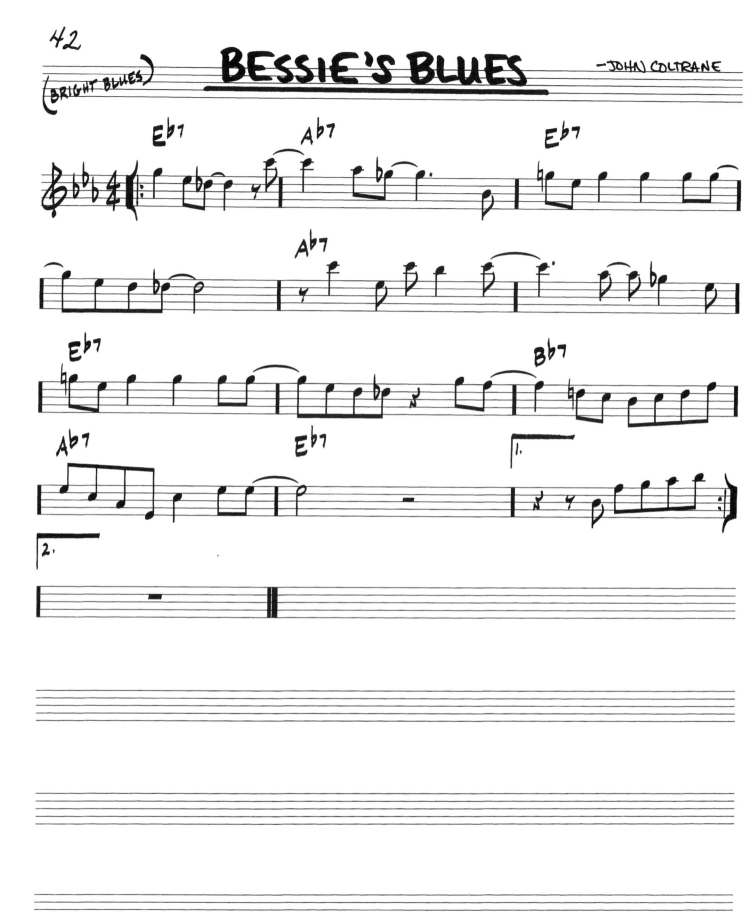

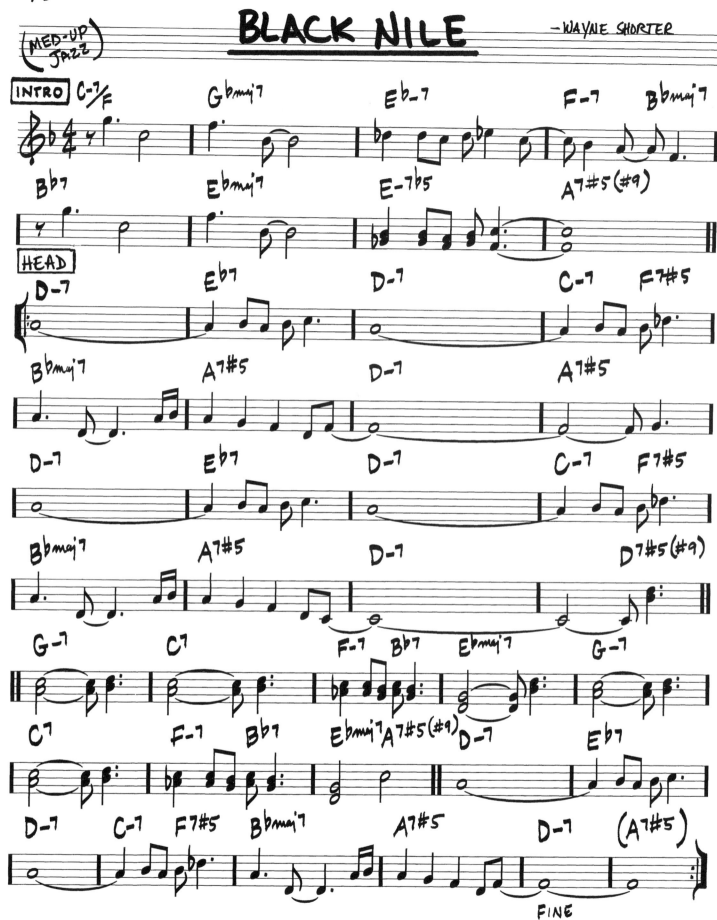

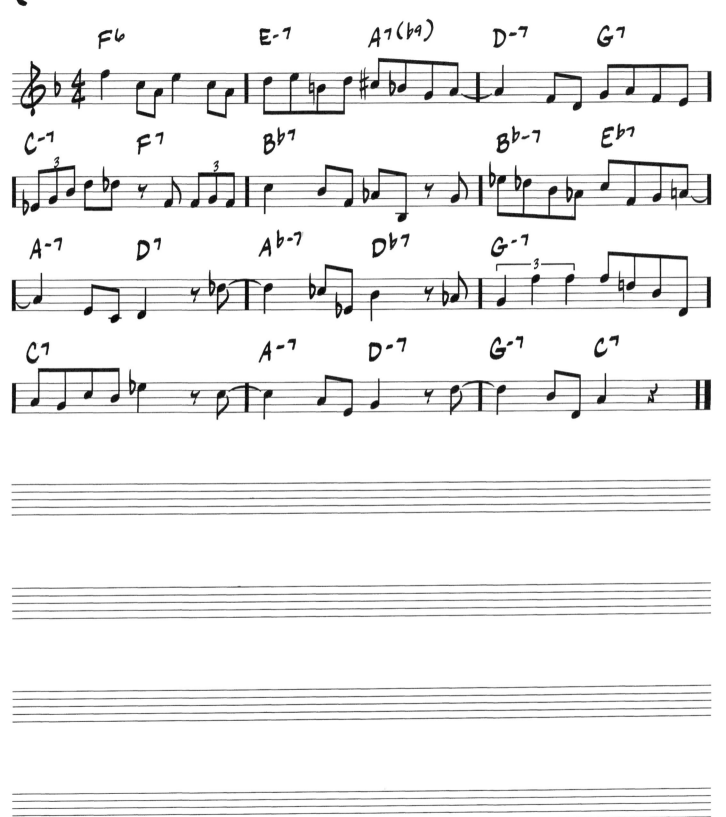

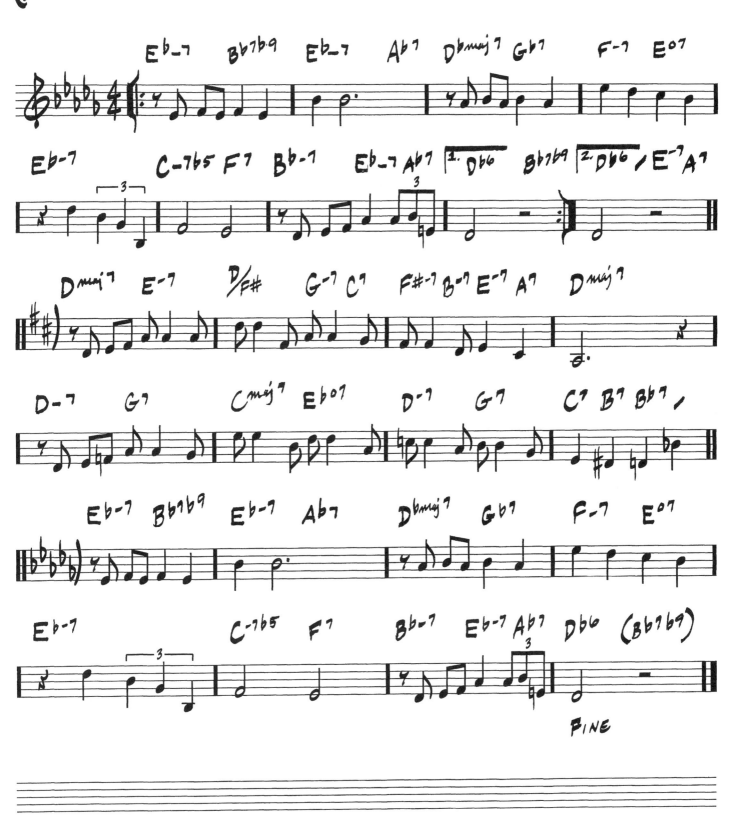

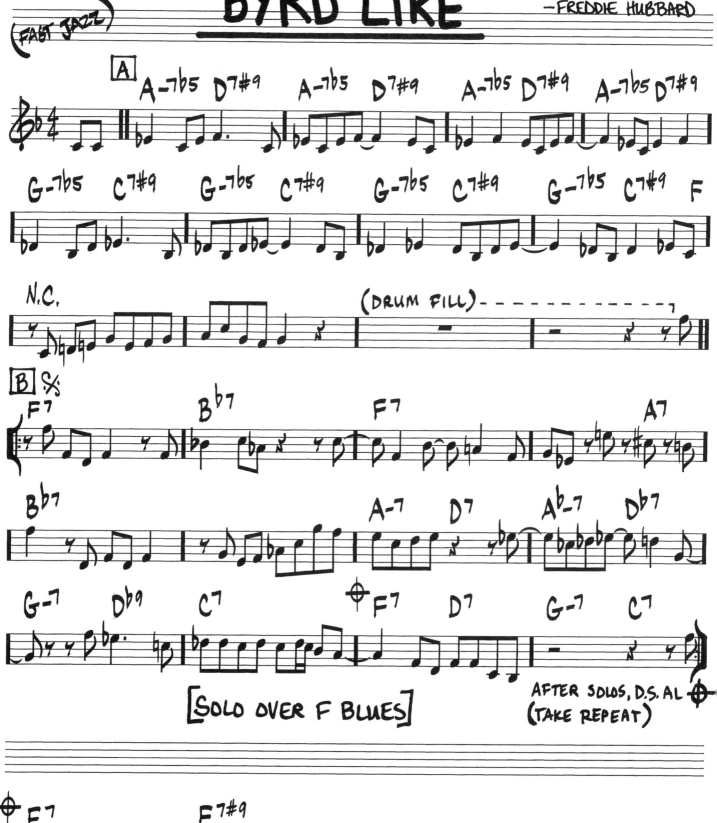

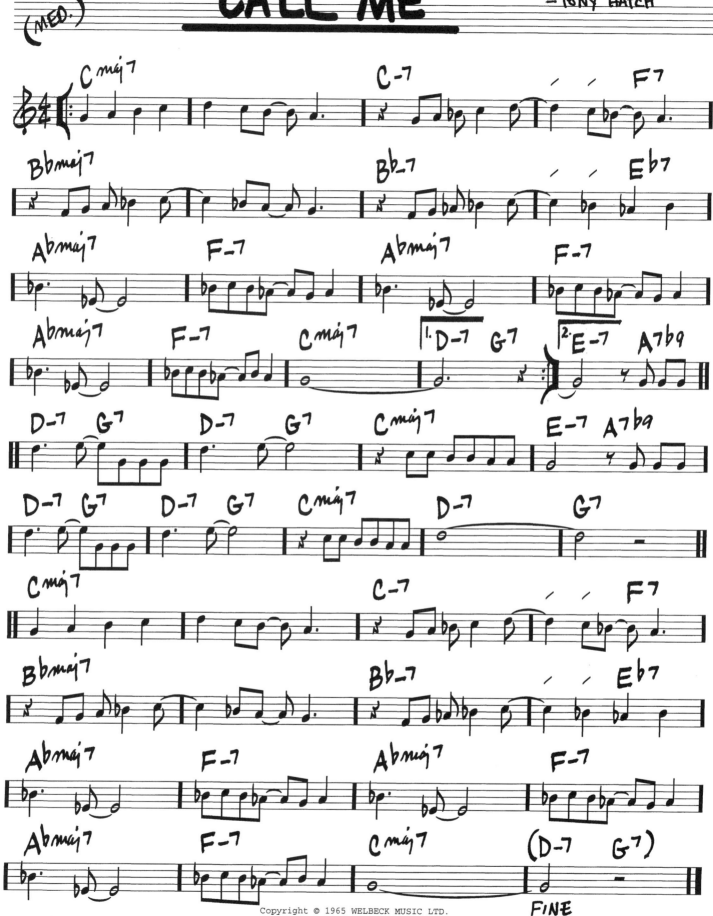

Can't Help Lovin' Dat Man

Jerome Kern / Oscar Hammerstein

(Ballad or Med.)

Key: Bb

Ebmaj7	C-7	F-7	Bb7	Ebmaj7	Bb-7 Eb7	Abmaj7	Db7
G-7	C-7	B7	B7#5 Bb7	**1.** Eb6	C-7	F-7	Bb7
2. Eb6		Bb-7 Eb7	Ab6		A°7		
Eb/Bb	C7	F7	F#°7	G-7	C7b9	F-7	F7
F-7/Bb		Bb7		Ebmaj7	C-7	F-7	Bb7
Ebmaj7	Bb-7 Eb7	Abmaj7	Db7	G-7	C-7	B7	Bb7#5 Bb7
Eb6	(C-7	F-7	Bb7)				

Cherry Pink and Apple Blossom White

(Bossa)

Loui Guy / Jacques LaRue / Mack David

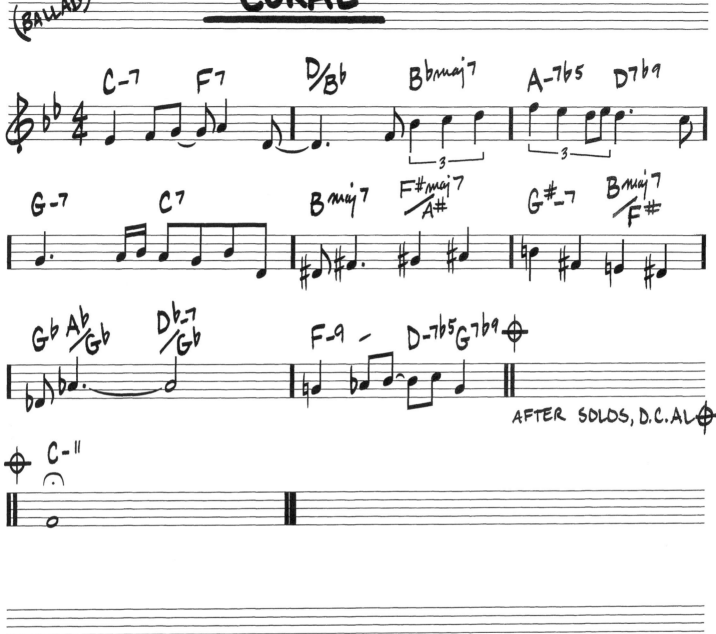

DAYS AND NIGHTS WAITING

— Keith Jarrett

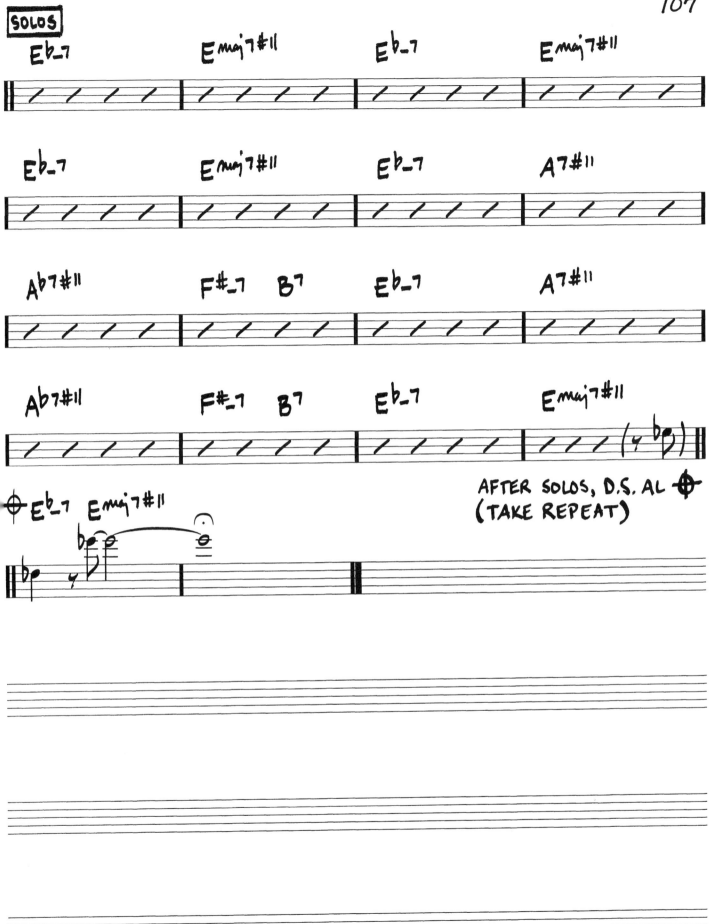

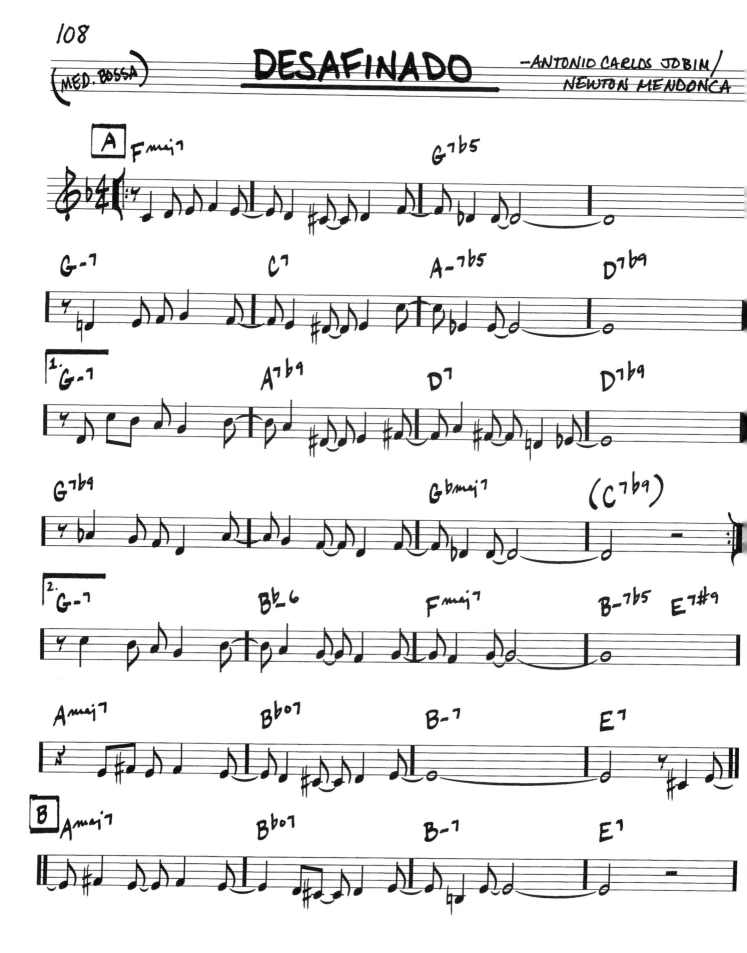

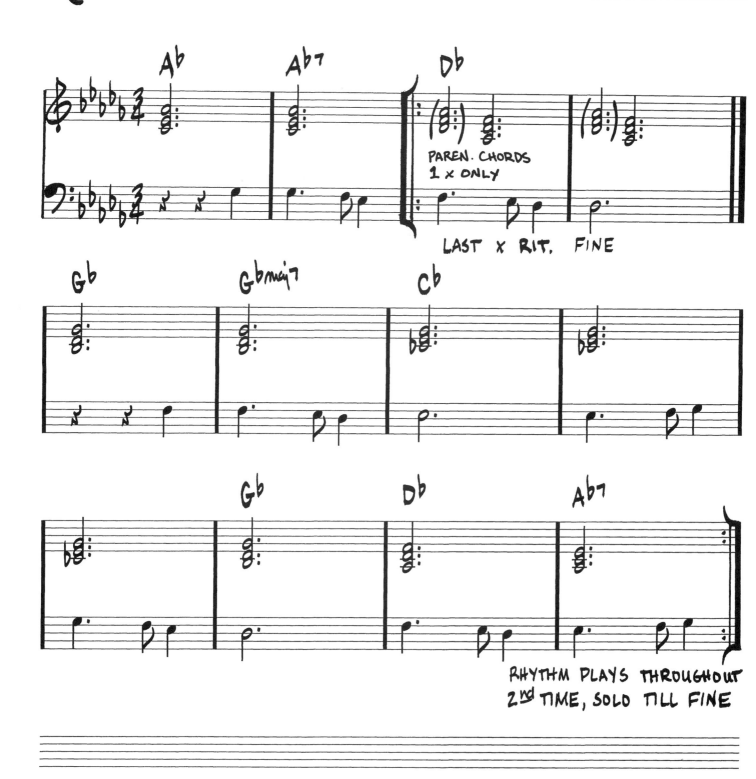

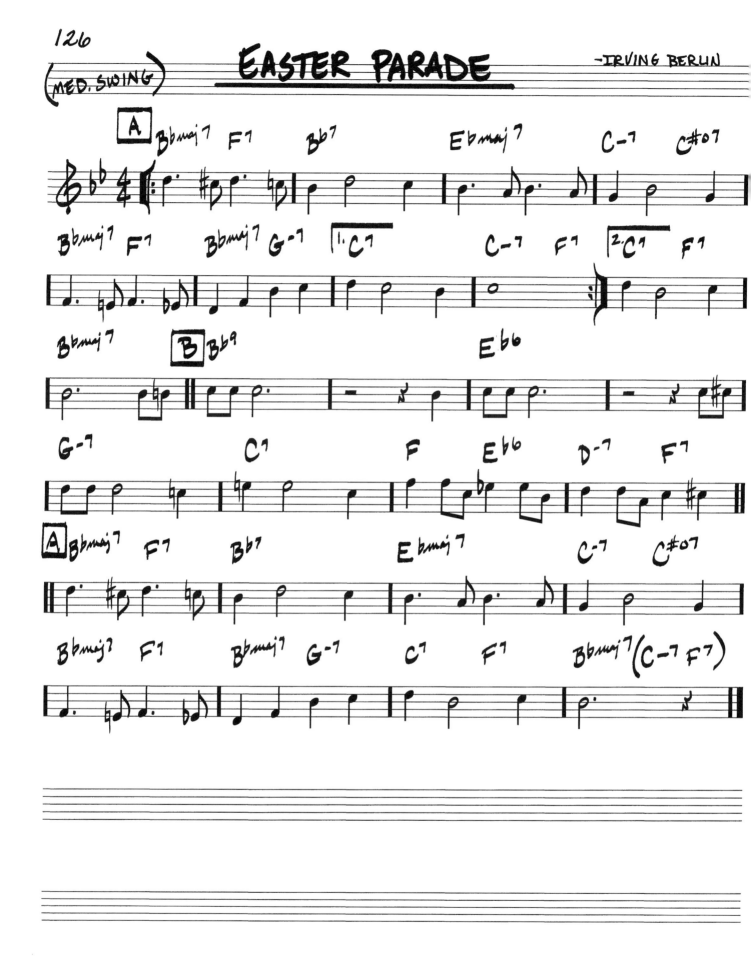

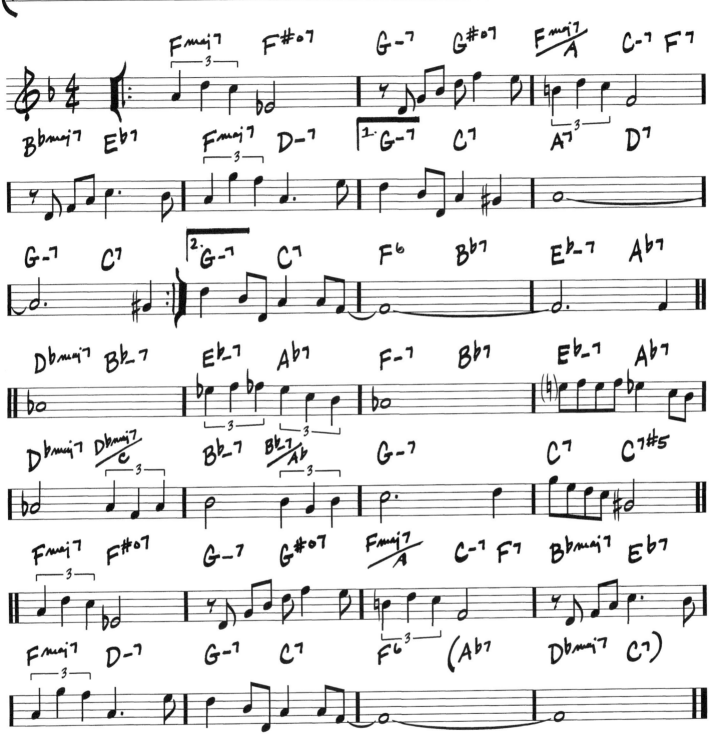

Falling In Love With Love

(Med. or Up)

— Richard Rodgers / Lorenz Hart

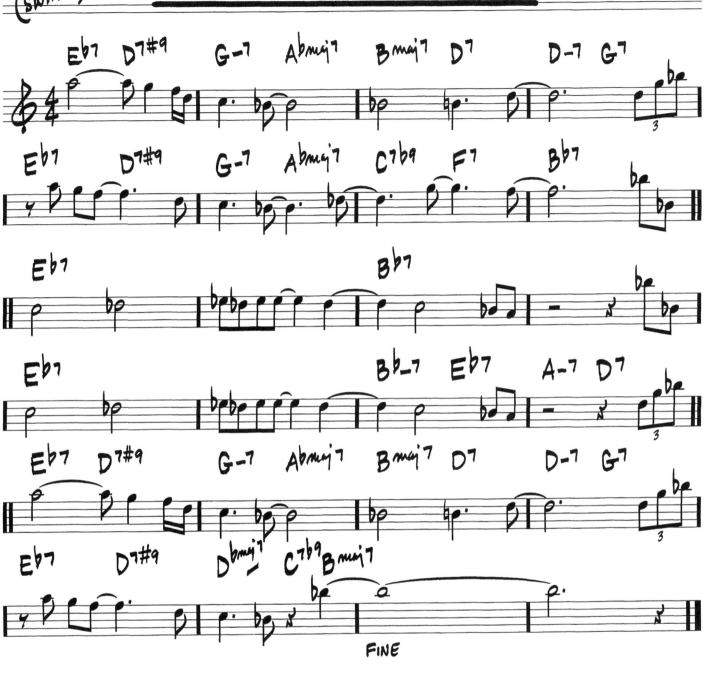

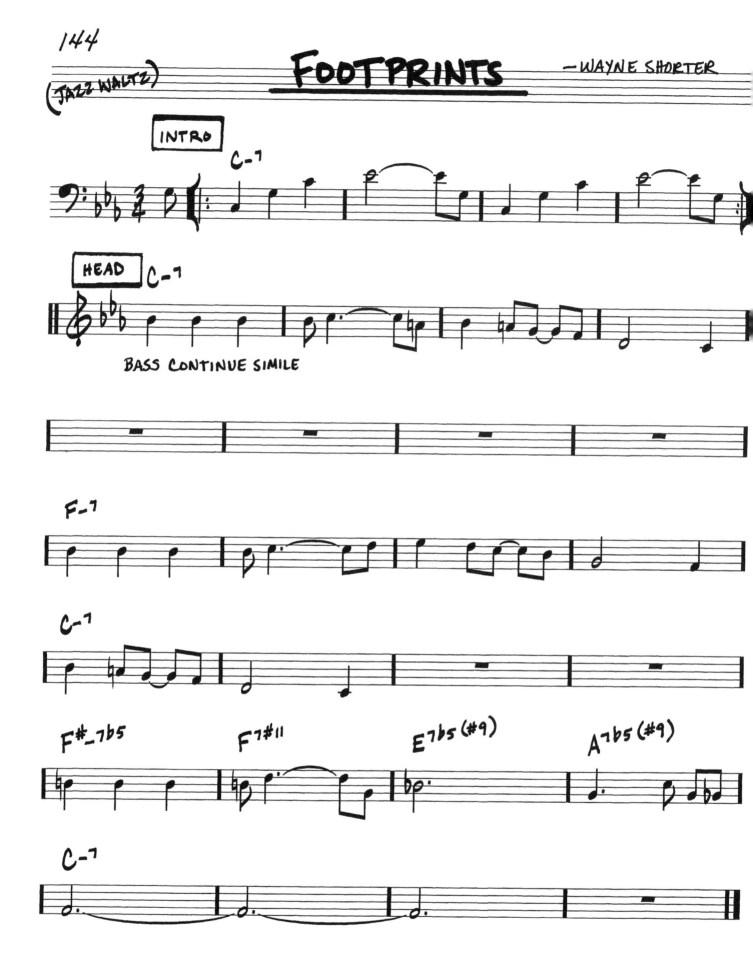

For Heaven's Sake

Four On Six

— John L. (Wes) Montgomery

150

(UP)

INTRO (BASS) N.C.

1.

2. B♭maj7 | G-7 G♯-7 A-7 | D7♯9 | N.C. |

HEAD G-7

1. C-7 | F7♯11 | B♭-7 | E♭7♯11 | A-7 | D7♯11 | E♭-7 | A♭7♯11 |

2. B♭maj7 | G-7 G♯-7 A-7 | D7♯9 | (SOLO BREAK) |

SOLOS G-7 | | C-7 F7 | B♭-7 E♭7 | A-7 D7 | E♭-7 A♭7 |

(4)

G-7 | | | C-7 F7 |

B♭maj7 | A-7♭5 D7♭9 | G-7 | A-7♭5 D7♭9 |

Copyright © 1960 (Renewed) by TAGGIE MUSIC CO., a division of Gopam Enterprises, Inc.

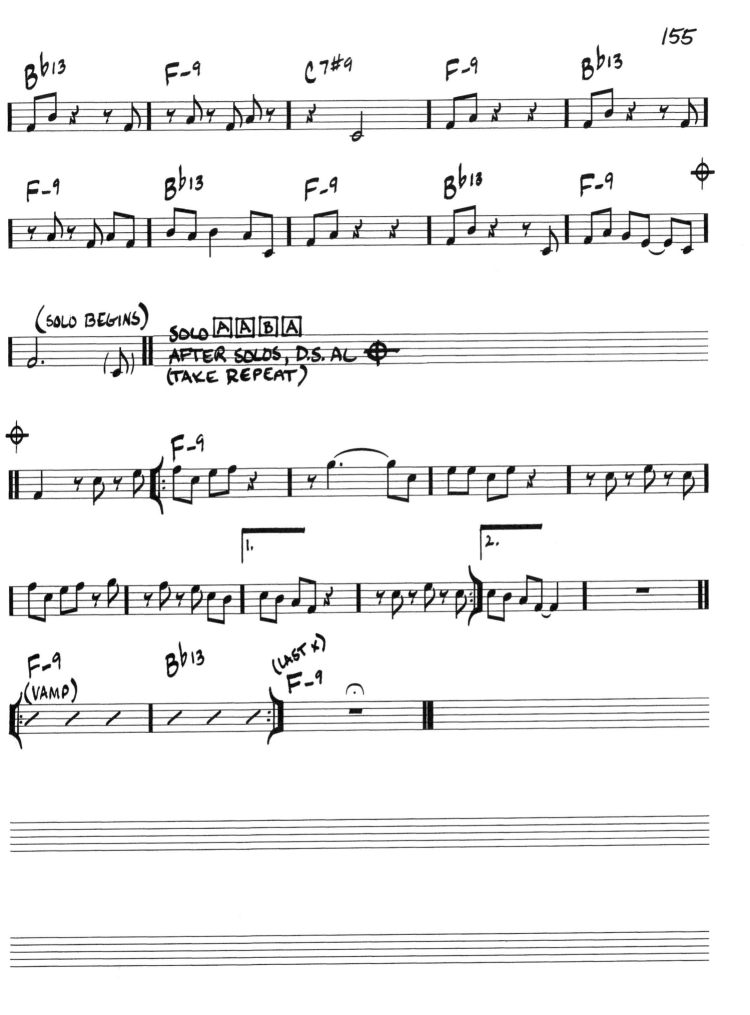

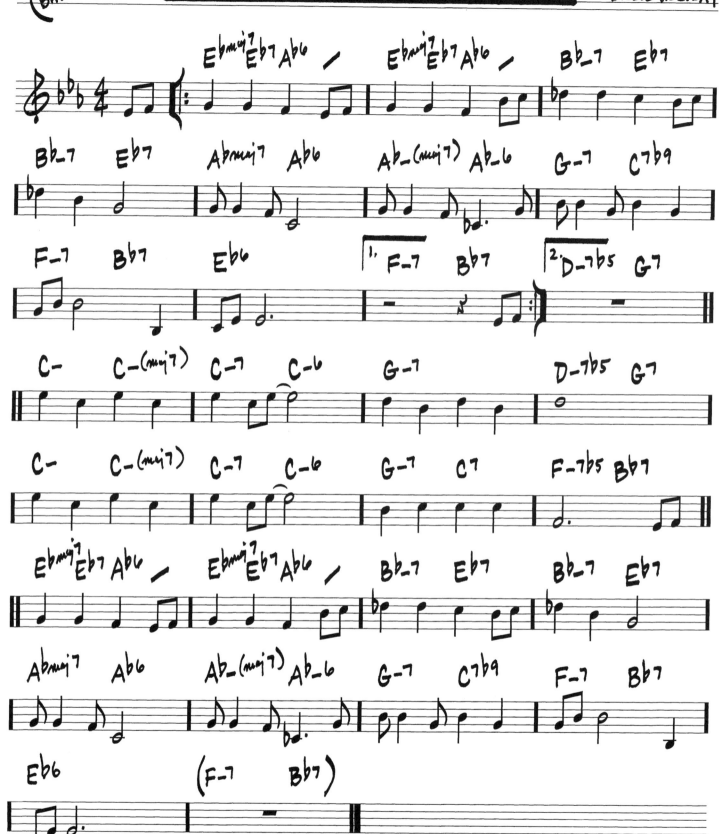

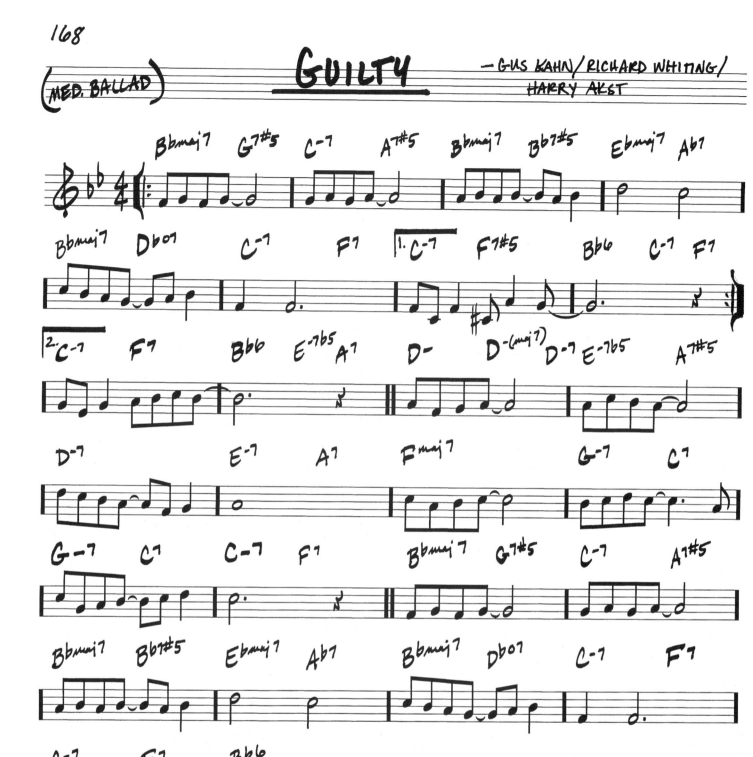

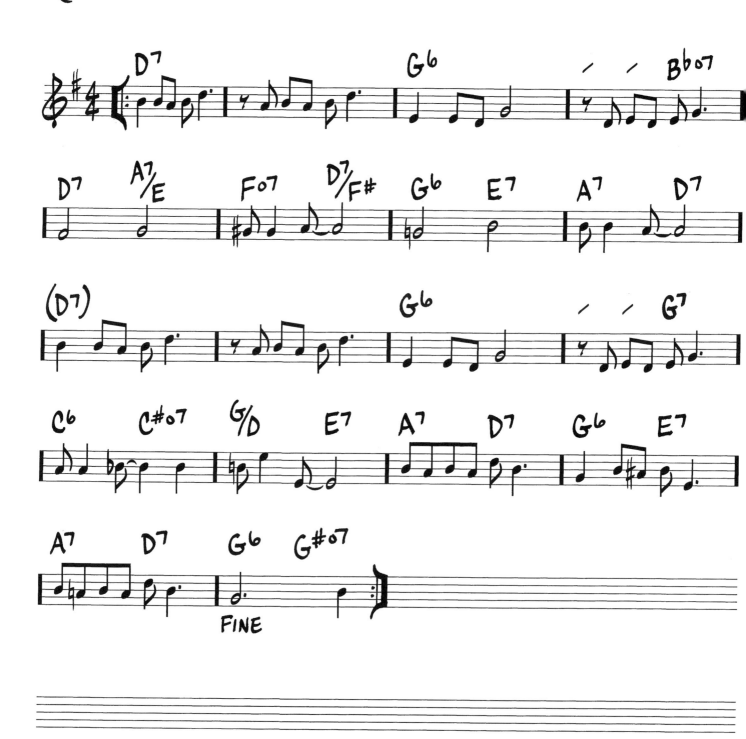

HERE'S THAT RAINY DAY

Jimmy Van Heusen / Johnny Burke

(Med.)

HOW INSENSITIVE
(INSENSATEZ)
— Antonio Carlos Jobim / Vinicius De Moraes / Norman Gimbel

(Bossa)

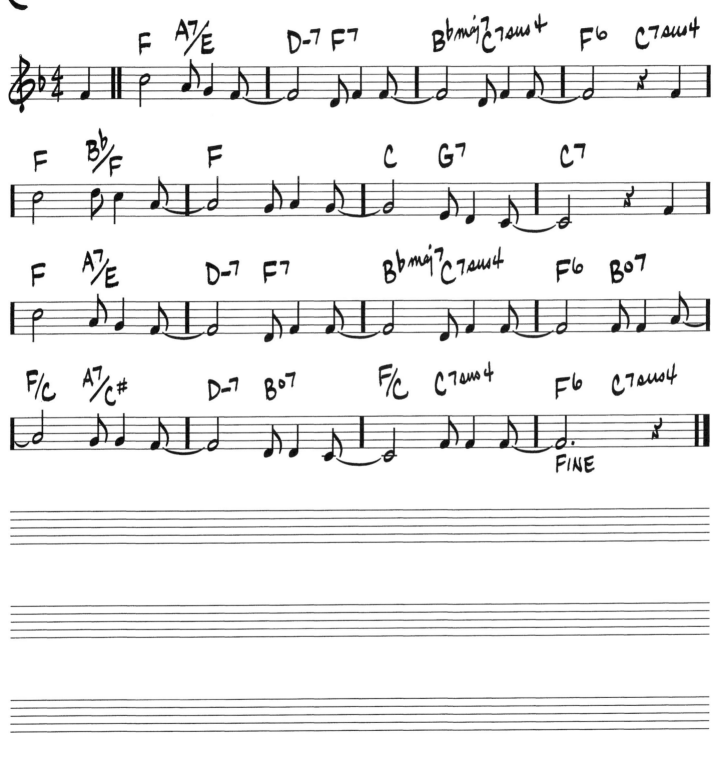

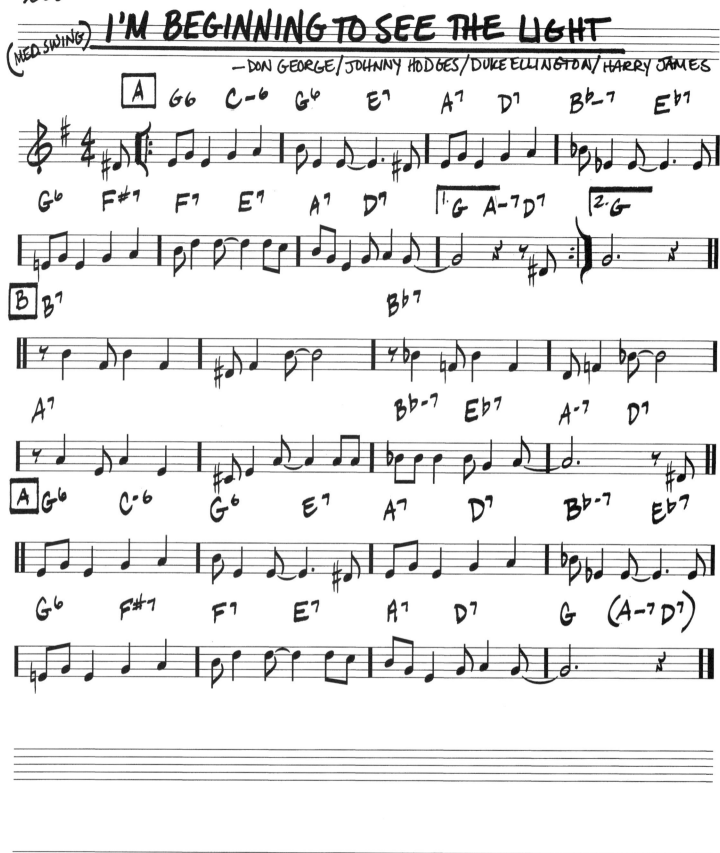

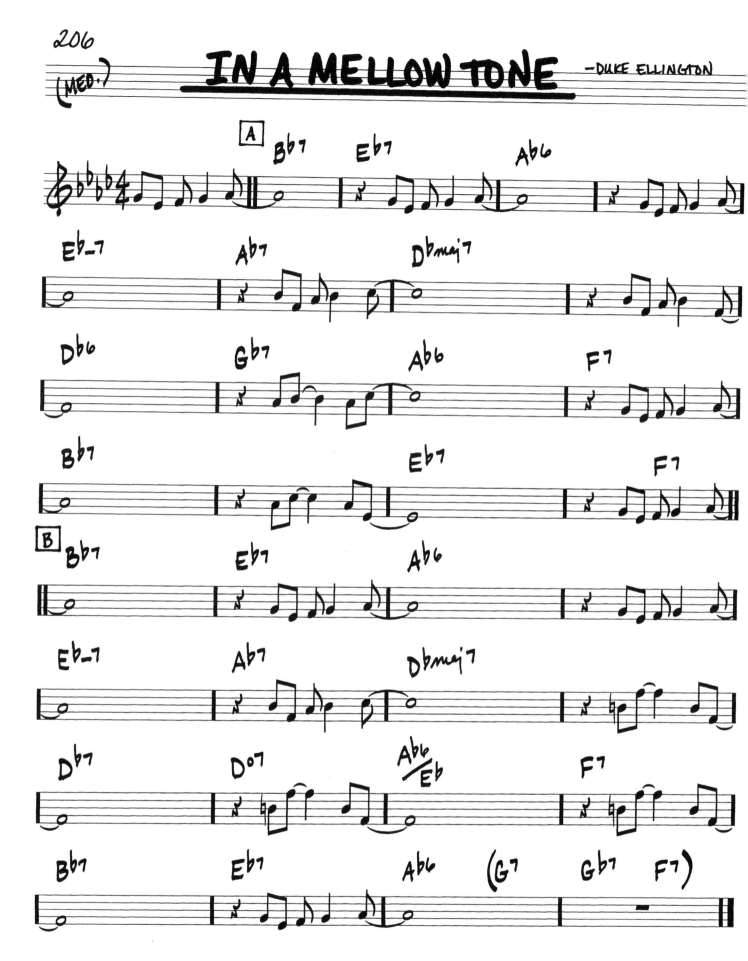

Jelly Roll

—Charles Mingus

(MED. 2 BEAT ♩=132)

For more than a snapshot version of Mingus, see Charles Mingus: More than a Fakebook (Hal Leonard)
Mingus website: www.mingusmingusmingus.com

Copyright © 1975 (Renewed 2003) JAZZ WORKSHOP, INC.

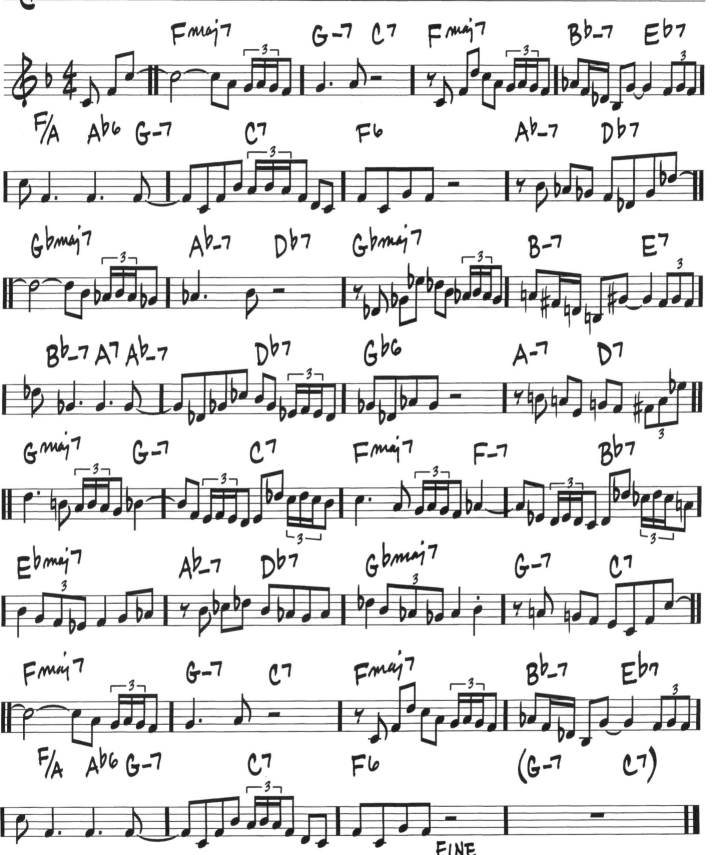

Lady Sings the Blues

(Slow Blues)

— Herbert Nichols / Billie Holiday

Las Vegas Tango

— Gil Evans

(EVEN 8ths)

FINE

AFTER SOLOS, D.C. AL FINE
(TAKE REPEAT)

Copyright © 1964 (Renewed 1992) BOPPER SPOCK SUNS MUSIC

LIKE SOMEONE IN LOVE
(Med.)

—Jimmy Van Heusen/Johnny Burke

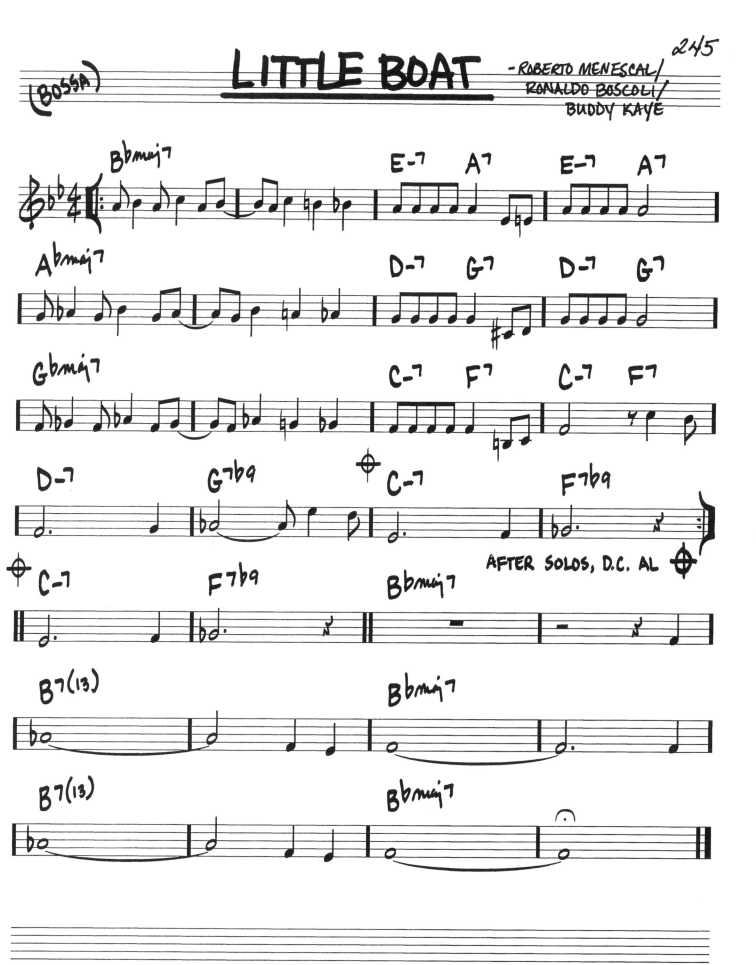

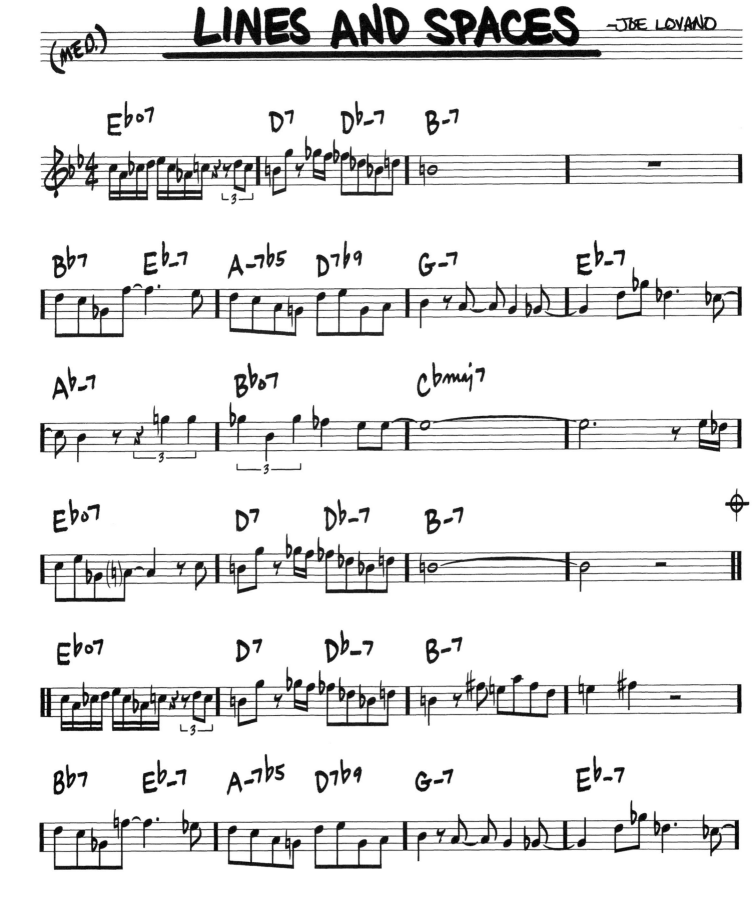

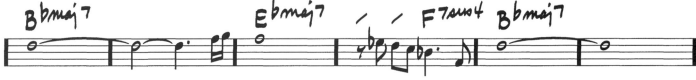

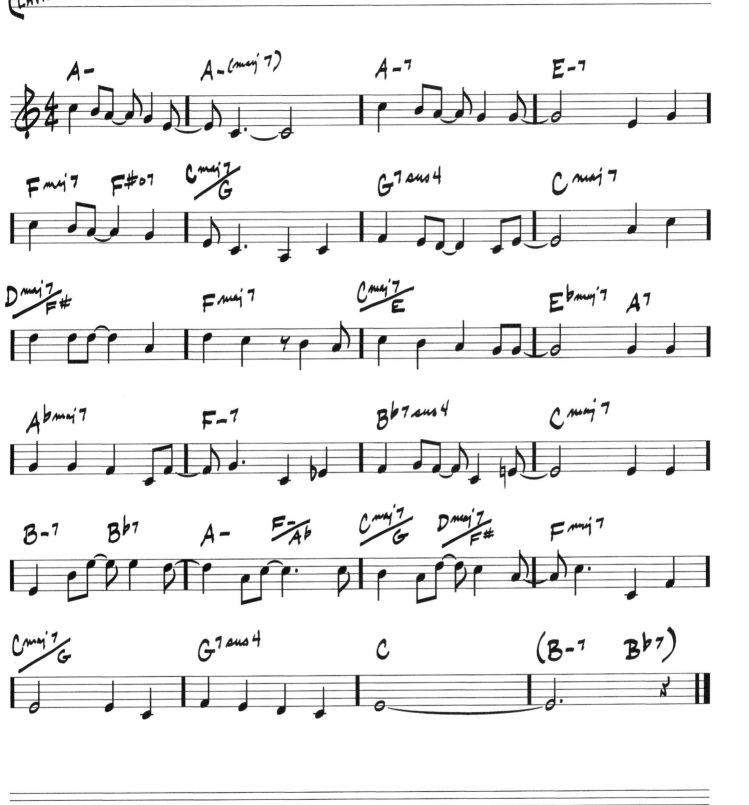

MR. P.C.
— John Coltrane

(BRIGHT JAZZ)

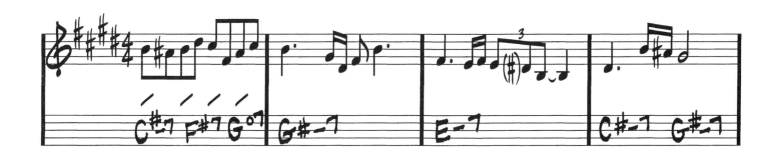

HEAD PLAYED ONCE — THEN TO SOLOS
LAST SOLO, D.C. AL ⊕

LAST TIME, TO OPEN SOLOS IN 4/4 ON F#-7
AFTER SOLOS, FADE W/ DRUMS

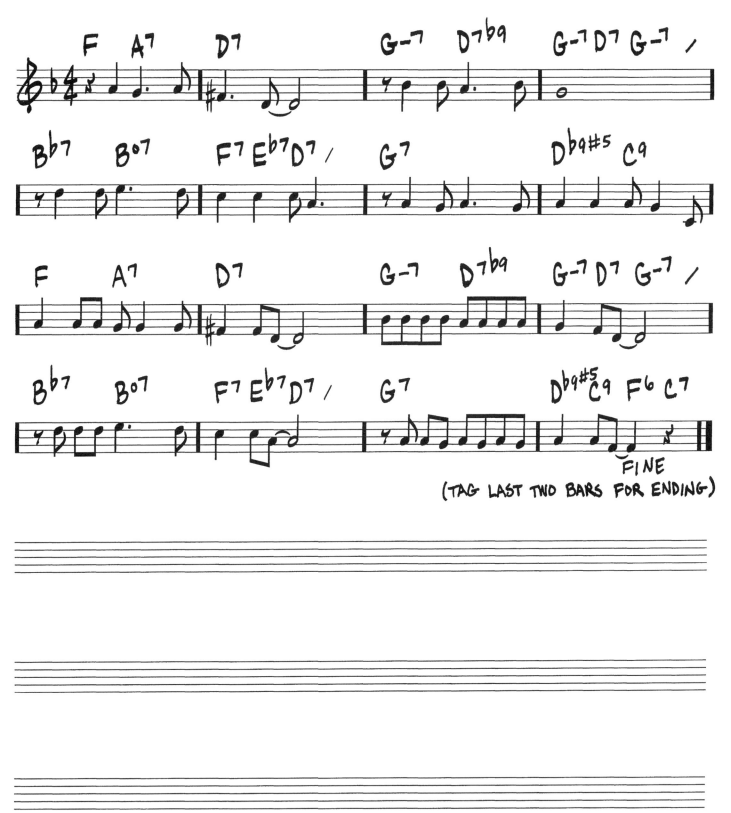

ADDITIONAL SOLOS 12-BAR BLUES
AFTER SOLOS, D.C. AL ⊕

(Old Man From) The Old Country

Nat Adderley / Curtis R. Lewis

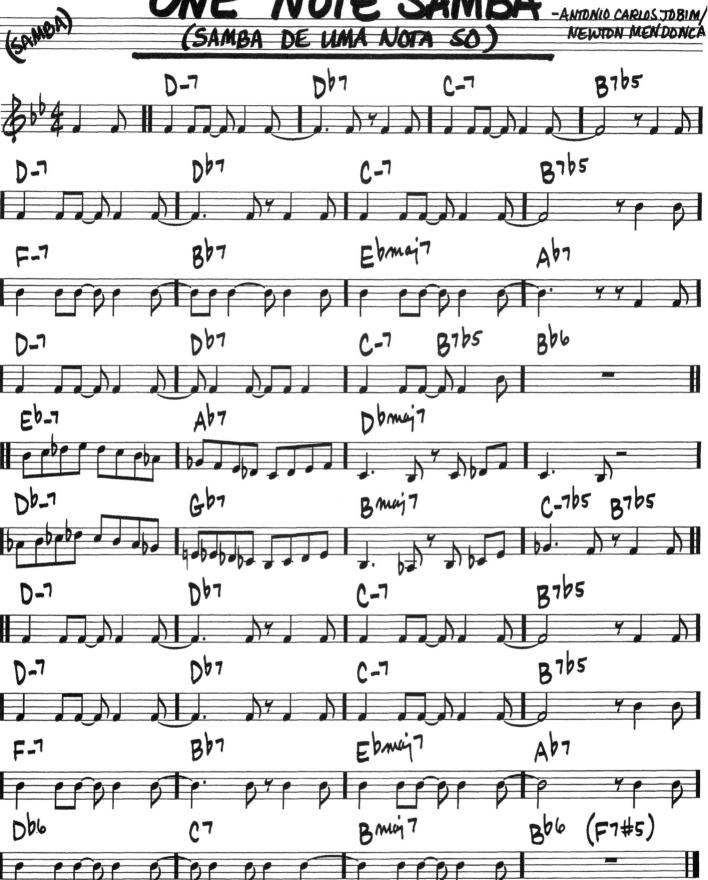

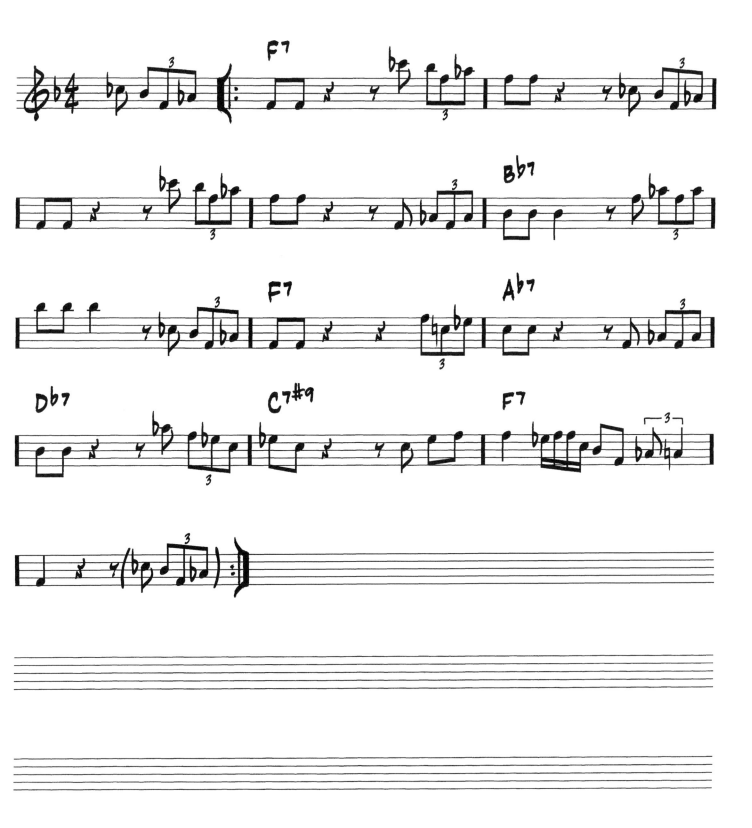

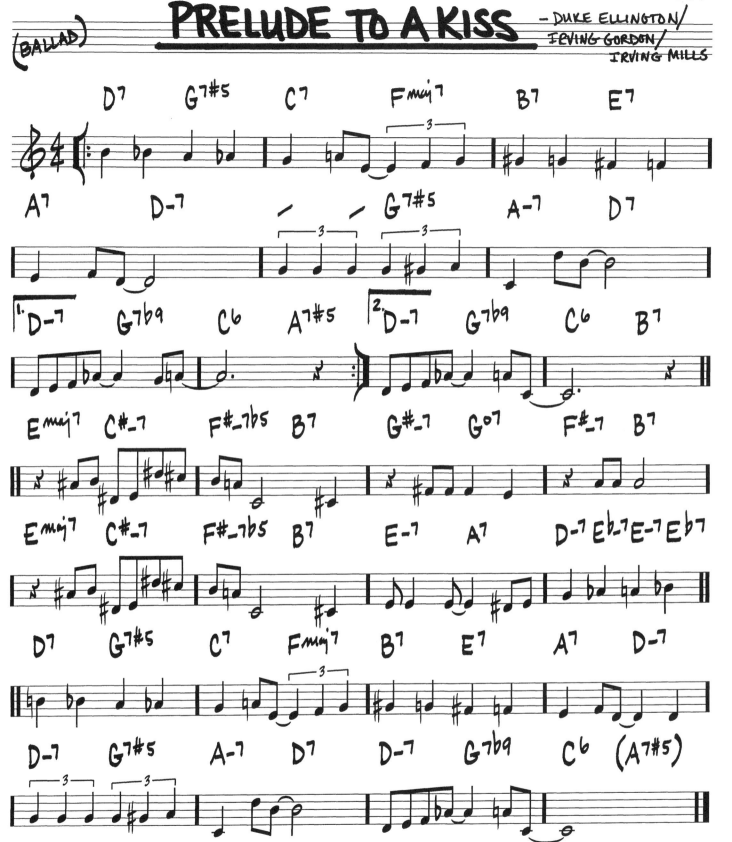

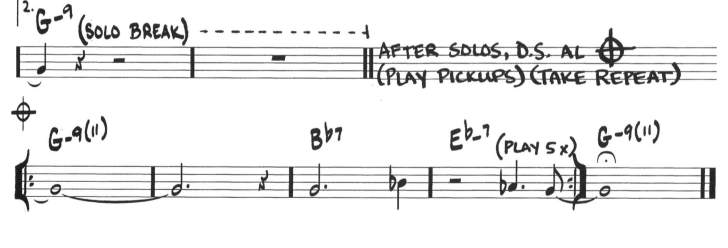

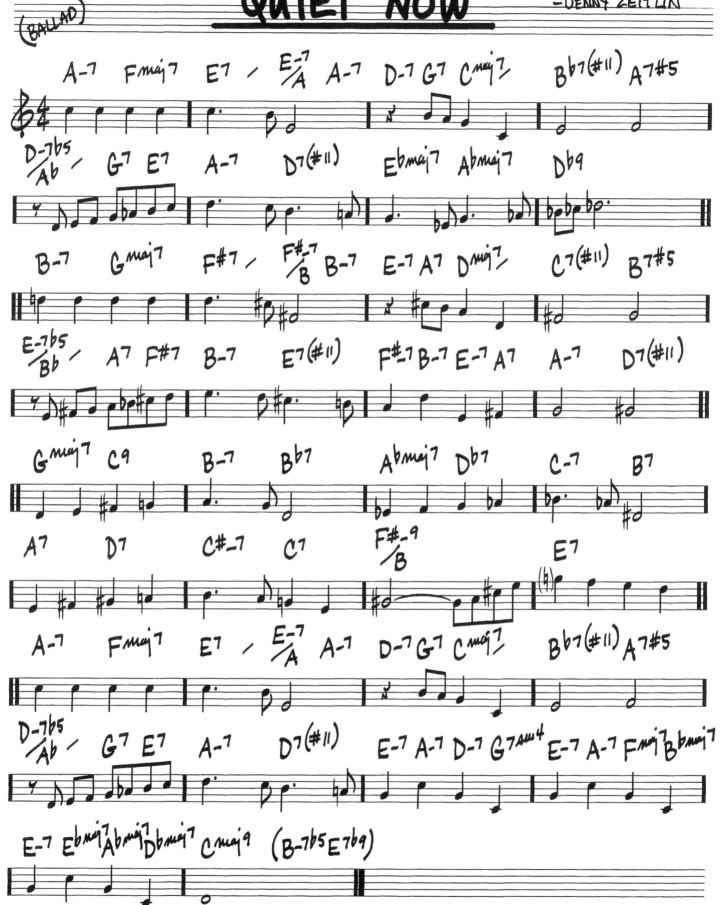

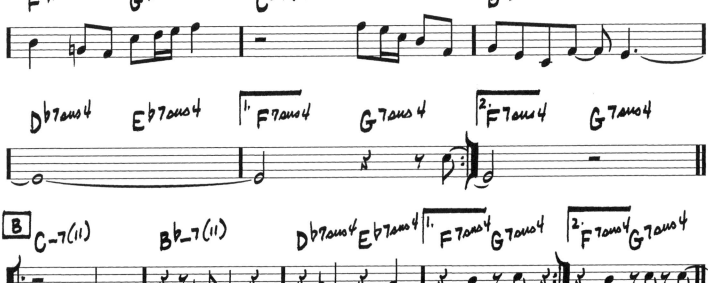

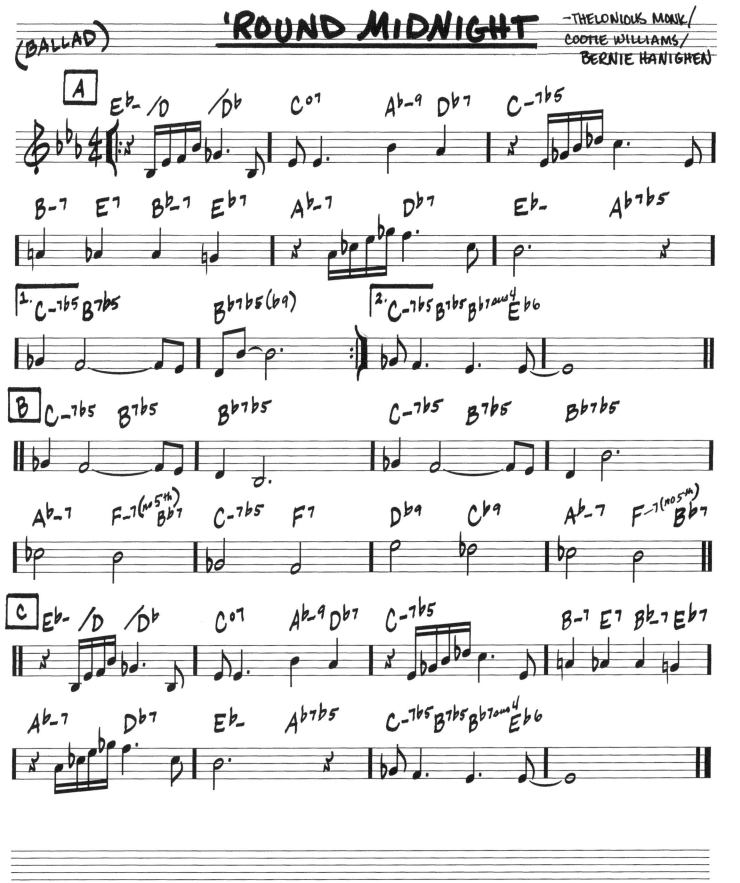

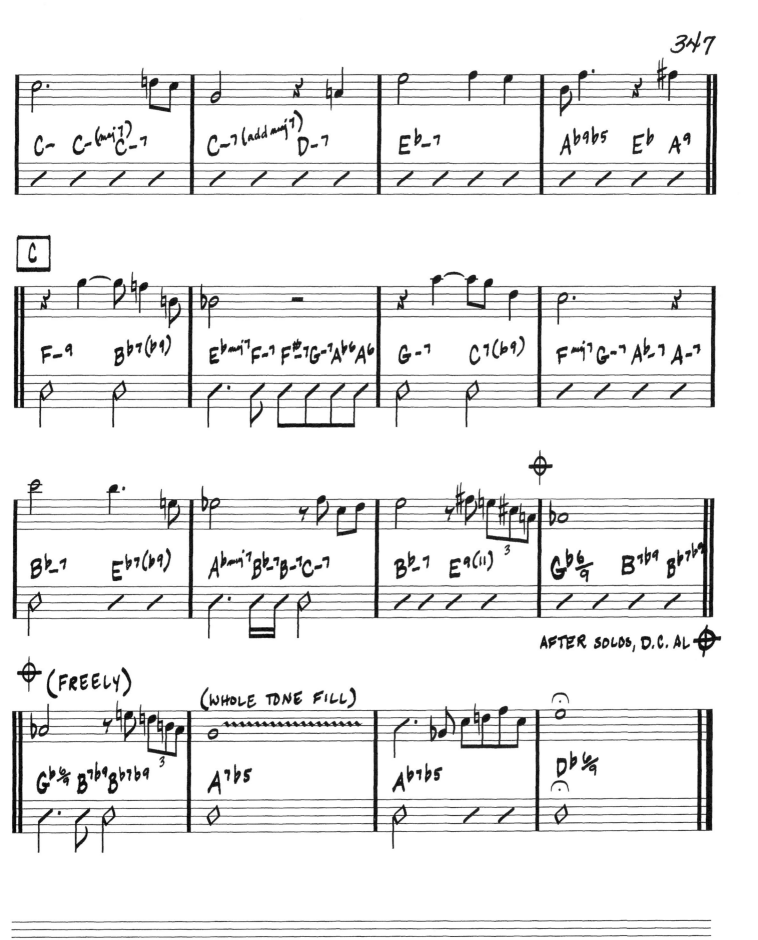

The Saga of Harrison Crabfeathers

Steve Kuhn

(Jazz Waltz)

348

Skating in Central Park

— John Lewis

(Med.)

Sheet music — lead sheet in 3/4

Copyright © 1959 (Renewed 1987) by MJQ Music, Inc.

After solos, D.C. al ⊕

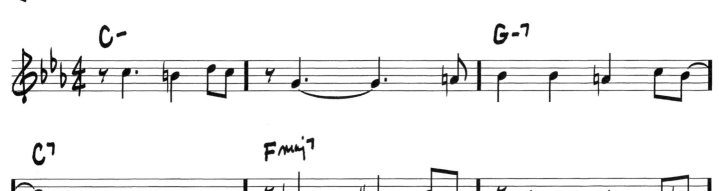

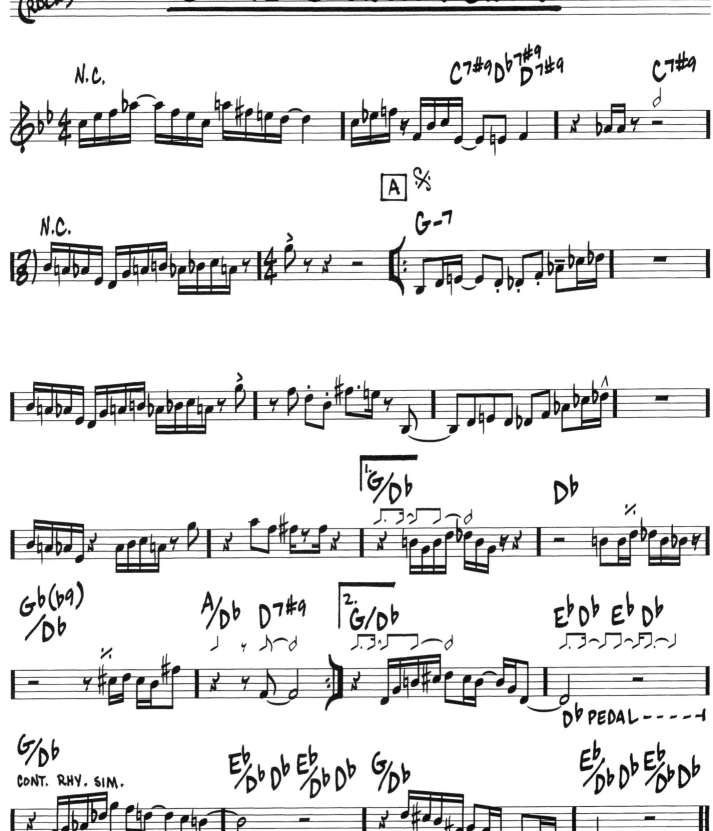

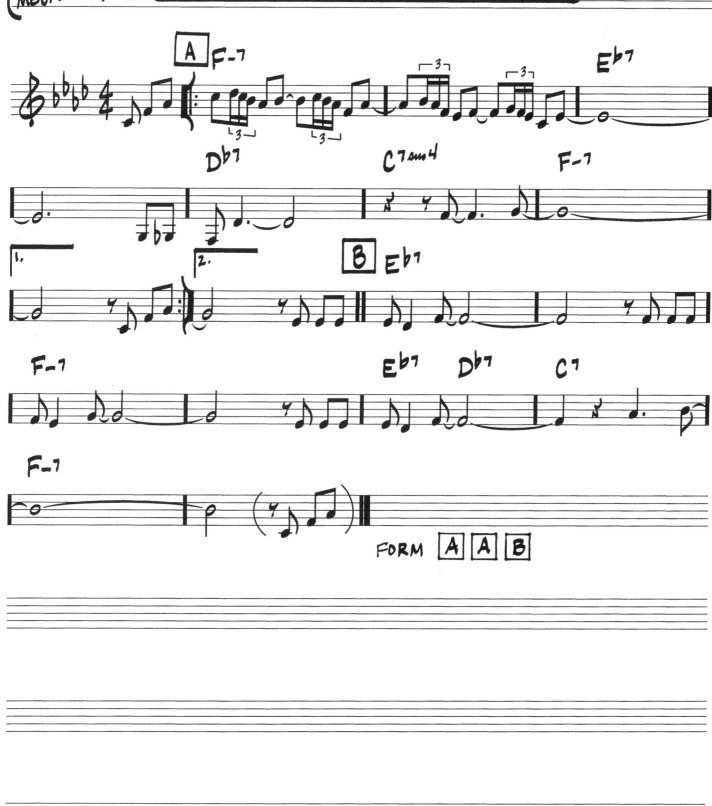

Sophisticated Lady

376
(Ballad)
— Duke Ellington / Irving Mills / Mitchell Parish

Copyright © 1933 (Renewed 1960) and Assigned to Famous Music Corporation and EMI Mills Music Inc. in the U.S.A.
Rights for the world outside the U.S.A. Controlled by EMI Mills Music Inc. (Publishing) and Warner Bros. Publications Inc. (Print)

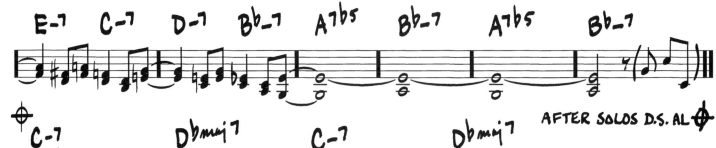

STANDING ON THE CORNER

(MED.)

-FRANK LOESSER

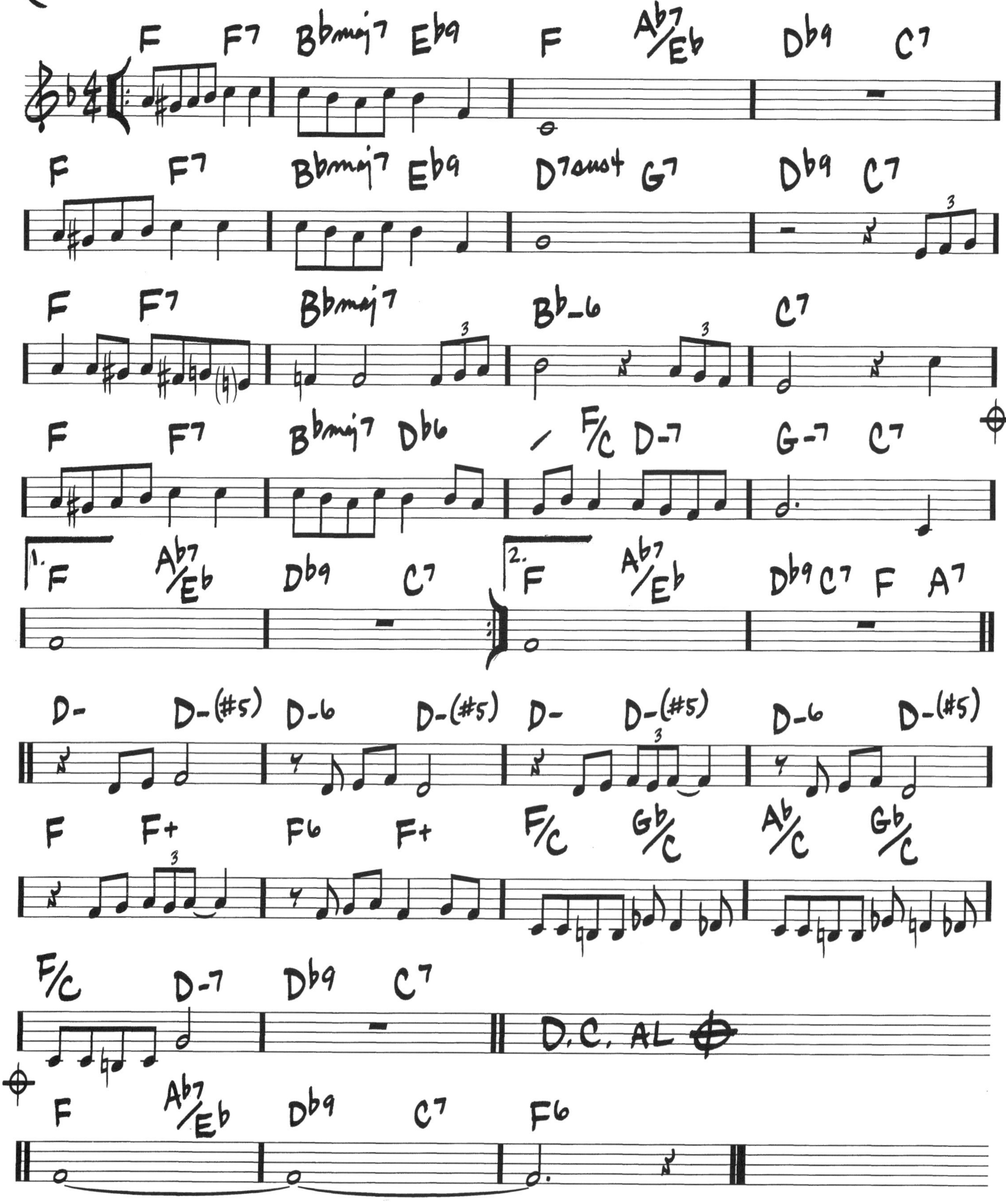

STEPS

— Chick Corea

(Fast Jazz)

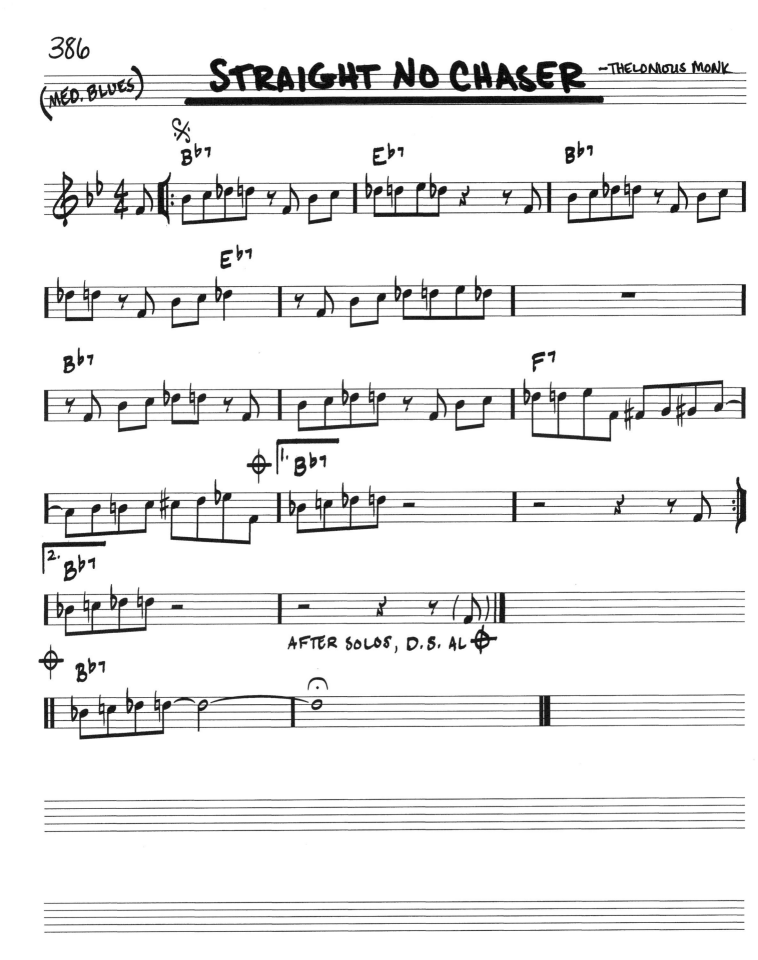

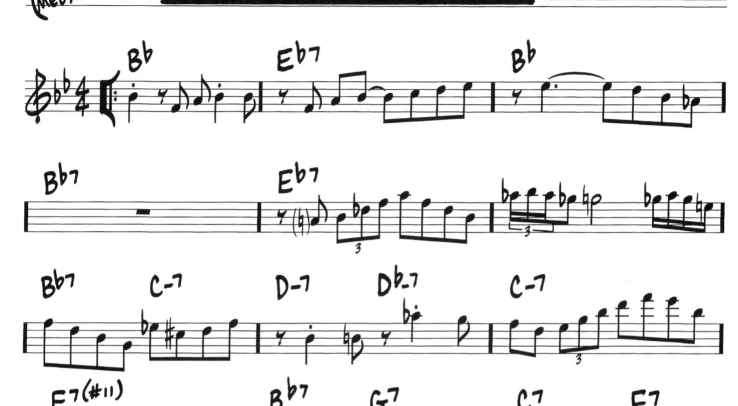

There Will Never Be Another You

— Harry Warren / Mack Gordon

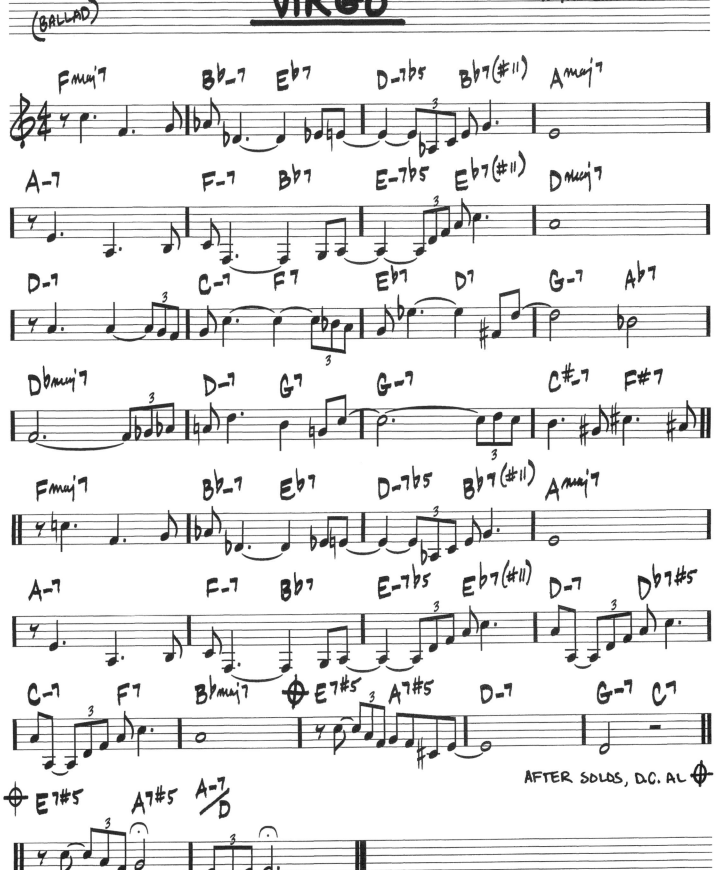

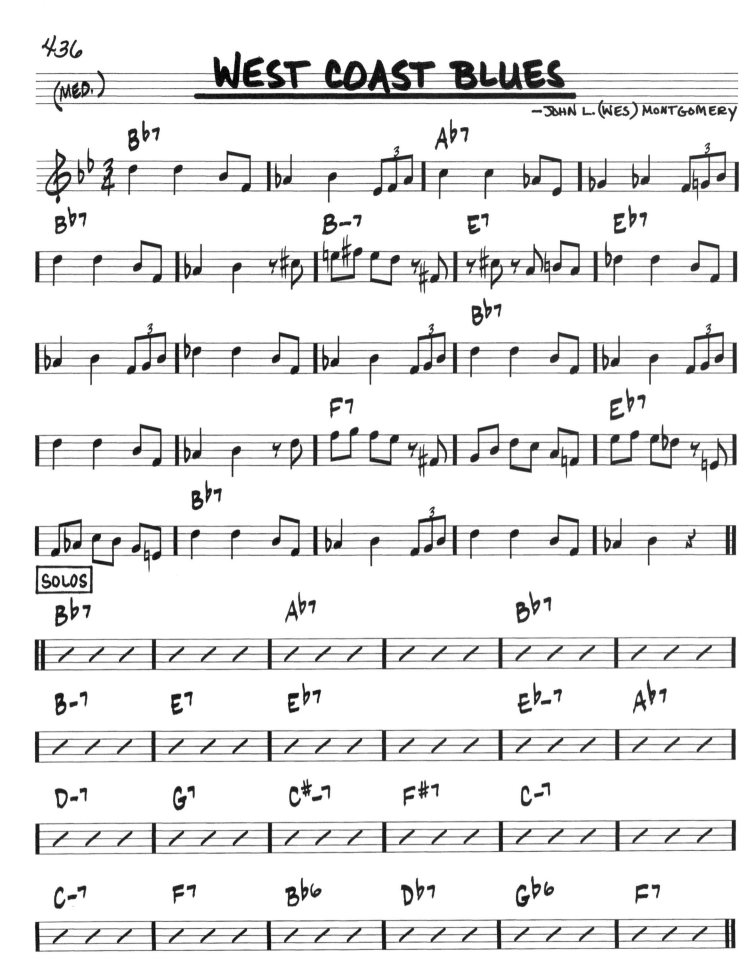

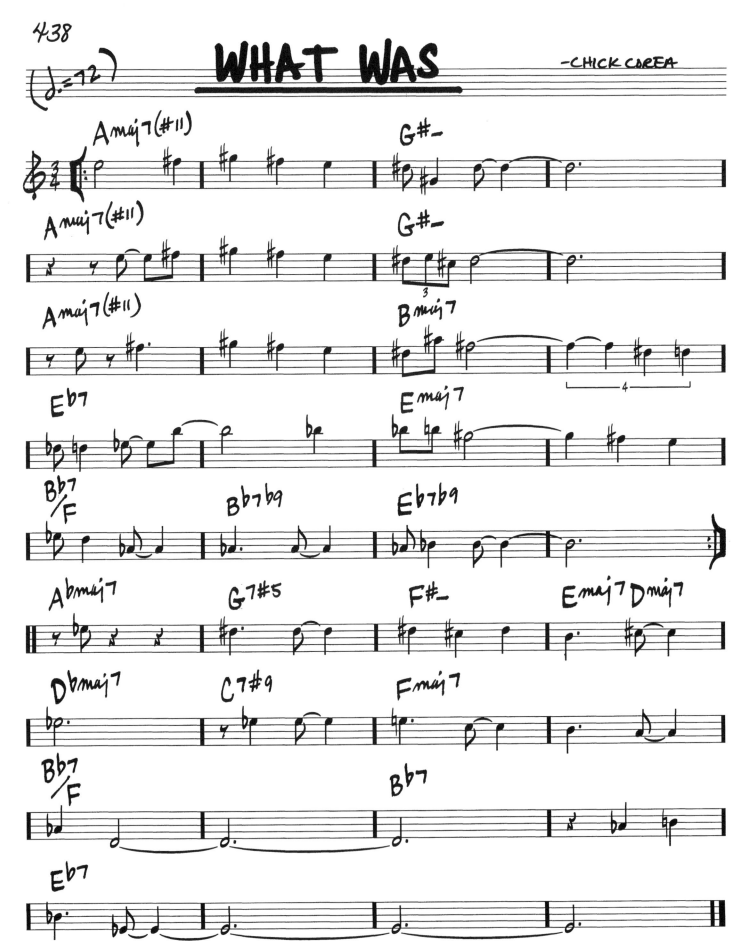

The World Is Waiting For The Sunrise

(Med.)

— Ernest Seitz / Eugene Lockhart

C6	G7#5	C6	E7
F F#o7	E-7 A7	D7	D-7 G7
C6	G7#5	C6	E7
F F#o7	E-7 A7	D-7 G7	C6

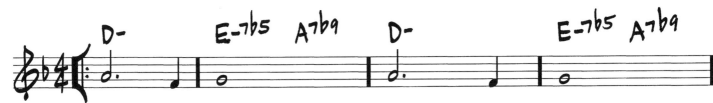
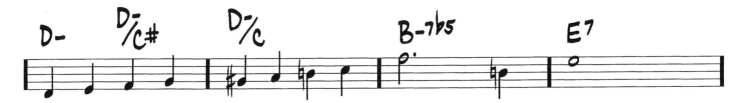

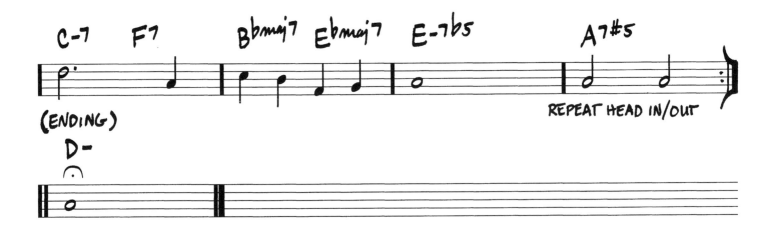

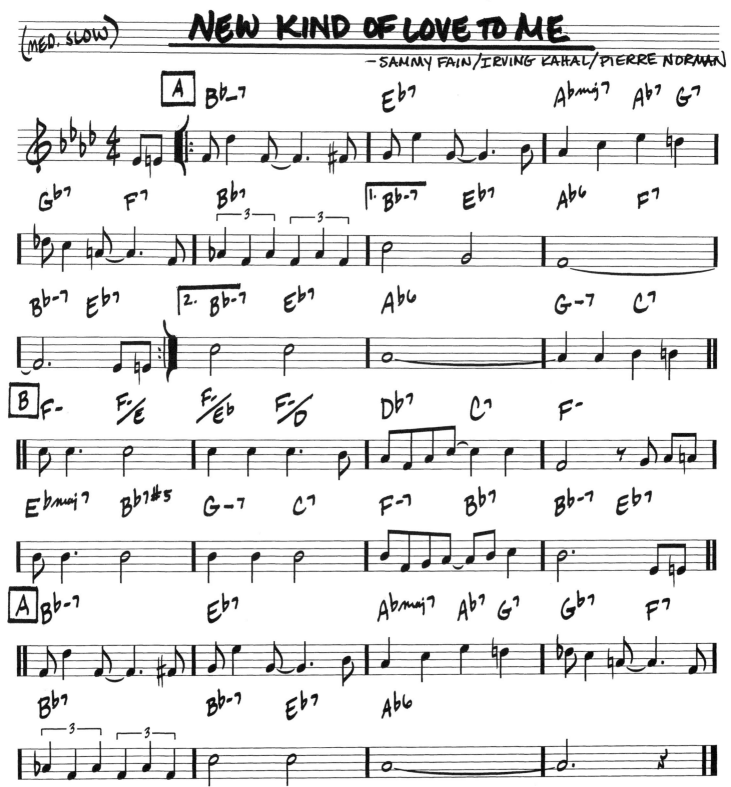

ALSO AVAILABLE

The Real Book – Volume 2

The Real Book – Volume 3

C, B♭, E♭ & Bass Clef Editons

More editions coming soon.

See your music dealer to order.

7777 W. BLUEMOUND RD. P.O. BOX 13819 MILWAUKEE, WI 53213

Visit Hal Leonard Online at
www.halleonard.com